WALKING A SOULFUL PATH

A HEALING JOURNEY WITH ANIMALS

FIONA SUTTON

Copyright 2024 © Fiona Sutton. First published in the UK by Amazon. Fiona Sutton asserts the right to be identified as the author of this work. All rights reserved. No parts of this publication may be reproduced, stored in a retrieval system, or transmitted in any form, or by any means, electronic, mechanical, photocopying, recording or otherwise without the prior permission of the author.

This is a work of non-fiction. The events and experiences detailed herein are true and have been faithfully rendered as the author has remembered them as to the best of her ability.

All the profits from the sale will go to the Gem shop and Holistic Centre for the care and welfare of their feral cats.

Table of Contents

Acknowledgments	3
Author's Note to Text	8
Introduction	9
The Awakening	13
PART 1 – ANIMALS AS TEACHERS	28
Jazz: A lesson in Soul purpose	31
Harry: A lesson in respect and spiritual growth	57
Silver: A lesson in Joy	68
PART 2 – ANIMALS GIVEN SECOND CHANCES	85
Watson: A lesson in transformation	89
Max: A lesson in the power of love	105
Tinkerbell: A lesson in honouring another's journey	124
PART 3 – SENTIENT ANIMALS	137
Annie: A lesson in acceptance	142
Prince: A lesson in trust and non-judgement	155
Ivor: A lesson in boundary setting	174
Rosie: A lesson in taming the ego	187
PART 4 – ANIMALS IN SPIRIT	198
Candy: Signs delivered from the other side	201
Tiffany: Help from the other side	218
Tess: A kiss from the other side	230
Afterword – Awaken the Magic	241
About the Author	251

Acknowledgements

My deepest and sincerest gratitude goes to all those people who have supported me in writing this book. I am indebted to family and friends for their assistance in editing the book, and for their honest feedback.

I owe my reiki teacher, Helen Courtney, a big thank you for her massive support and encouragement on my spiritual path; empowering me to achieve things beyond my wildest dreams. Her unwavering support and belief in me has enabled me to trust and have faith in something which just seemed impossible. I am truly indebted to Helen for awakening my belief in myself.

Another earth angel I am so grateful to is Jenny Smedley, renowned spiritual healer, author and artist, for the beautiful cover of my book. I feel truly honoured that my book depicts her incredible artwork.

I am also incredibly grateful to my book coach, Katie Oman, who has helped me to edit and birth this book into the world. Without her, it would never have happened. Thank you, Katie, for your incredible patience and kindness. I know my tech skills (or lack of them) test the patience of a saint!

Another person to whom I owe a huge debt of gratitude is Hannah Cooper. Her beautiful pencil drawings grace the start of each chapter, and she has faithfully depicted the wonderful souls of the animals through her drawings. These really enhance the book, in my opinion.

A big thank you must also go to my dad and my two children for encouraging me and helping in the editing of the book. I am also indebted to my husband for his unfailing support; made more notable by the fact that he does not share my spiritual beliefs.

Last but not least, this book would not have been birthed if it wasn't for the incredible animals and their equally wonderful Humans, who allowed me into their lives, entrusting me with my Animal Communication work and reiki healing skills. My gratitude is off the scale for these amazing souls. There is so much to take away from their lessons and teachings. They truly can help us become better Humans.

Thank you to everyone who has bought this book. Please lend this book to someone you know who will appreciate it. Even better, please buy them a copy. The profits from the sale of the book will go to help the many feral cats who are being cared for by the Gem Gift shop and holistic centre (part of the Halfpenny Green Vineyards, Bobbington).

Thank you all for loving animals and seeing their beautiful souls. Only love can make for a better world. Let's allow our animals to show us the way!

Oh great horse
If you could know
How your gifts have helped me grow.
Once I was lost, but now am found
Dancing free to your pure sound!

Oh great horse
You cannot see
How your heart has awakened me.
For now as I gaze deep within your soul
The treasures within have made me whole.

Oh great horse
If you could see
How your wisdom has enlightened me.
For knowledge alone is an empty thing
Requiring heart to make it sing.

Oh great horse
If you only knew
How my gratitude has grown for you.
Your magnificent heart has set me free
Bringing me home and back to me.

Oh great horse
My beloved friend
My heart and soul were yours to mend
Our souls entwined forever more
Binding our hearts at their core.

Oh great horse
Please forgive me
Your majestic Being I could not see
Hidden from view, yet in plain sight
It took a miracle to see your light.

Oh great horse
You hold the key
To awaken mankind, Humanity
Once we rode upon the Earth
Now we fly in our rebirth!

FIONA SUTTON

There are those amongst us
Who have never lost their way!
They are the ones who have never become
Seduced by power,
Dazzled by money,
Or overcome with greed.
Rather, they have remembered what is important,
Finding joy in the simple things;
The things that matter!
They are the ones who remember who they are
Retaining their sacredness
To the Earth and each other!
These are the ones to whom this book is dedicated.

Thank you animals for gracing our lives
Reminding us who we are
And to whom our responsibilities lie!
You are the guides to an awakening world!
Through your forgiveness and love
We can open our hearts
And find our way home.

This is the path to peace!

Author's Note to Text

As animals are not inanimate objects, and they do have gender, then in order to avoid using the pronoun "it" when referring to an animal, I have gone with convention and used "he."

I have also tried not to objectify animals by using the word "owner" when referring to the human side of an animal-human relationship. Instead, I use the term, the "animal's guardian."

I have also changed the names and identity of people and animals, when it seems appropriate to do so.

INTRODUCTION

For quite some months, the fringes of my awareness had contained the knowledge that I was to write a third book. I knew it would include Animal Communication and Reiki healing. These arts had become such an important part of my life, but the full content of the book just seemed to evade me and I couldn't get nearly excited enough to start putting pen to paper.

Magically, the Universe stepped in to rescue me. It was the 2021 winter Solstice. There was so much talk in spiritual circles regarding the divine light that was streaming into our consciousness, and there was much talk about ascension symptoms. The energy was supposedly intense!

My ears started to feel strange. I am not great at describing sensations, and this is no exception, so I won't even attempt to describe it. Intuitively, I just seemed to know that my ear chakras were opening. For two nights, I struggled to sleep, and the reason became obvious: I was receiving downloads from the Universe! The book I was to write appeared to me in crystal clear form. Not only was I aware of all the chapters to be included, but I could sense, feel and see the book in its completed form. More than anything, I just felt really excited about it, and the urgency was enough to make me start penning it.

Before you dismiss me as a complete madwoman, please just take the time to read the opening chapter. Once upon a time, I was a very different person, with different perceptions and views of life than what I have now. Events in March 2012 changed everything for me. My whole thought system was hung on the line like dirty washing. And rather than just letting it air, I decided to throw it away and take new stock. The truths that were now staring me in the face, made me question everything I had been taught and thought I knew. In the process, I dismantled my whole thought/belief system and went in search of answers relating to a very different truth. I was led down paths that I never knew existed, and I was able to find a very different way of navigating life - one that served me a whole lot better, where peace, love and joy were so much more accessible, and where fear could be put on the backburner.

My changed beliefs and the strength these brought me, were very much the subject matter for my first book, *"Seeker of the Light."*

I wanted to write a book about Animal Communication (AC) and Reiki healing, because these practices have been so much part of my life the last twelve years. But I wanted it to go beyond this, and not just tell the stories of animals who have experienced enormous transformations. The truth is that, although I have witnessed some unbelievable changes in the animals I have worked with, I have also come to recognize that AC and Reiki healing is a two way thing; it isn't just about the human helping the animal. On the contrary, there is a lot of healing coming from the animals themselves. They too have much to teach us, and they are incredible healers in their own right; so much so in fact, that I would go as far as to say that animals have been put on the planet to help us evolve.

This book features animals I have worked with, some of them my own. I have tried to focus on the animals who not only experienced some incredible transformations, but those whose stories have some very impactful messages and teachings for us. In their stories, there is a lot for us to learn and take away.

Animals have a very deep, soul underlay to them; one that our society chooses to ignore for the most part. This is probably because by so doing we can then use them for our own ends, without feeling guilty. Seeing them as *"just an animal"* helps excuse the lack of respect and our sometimes barbaric treatment of them, but in thinking this way we are losing out on the magical connections that are possible and the deep soul bonds we can form.

I believe that animals have many reasons for being with us here on Earth, and like us, I do believe that they have soulful purpose for entering our lives. For many of us they are a gift. They are like Earth angels, and many of us would have struggled with our lives on Earth without having an animal nestled in our heart. In them we have found our support team; our friends, cheerleaders, as well as teachers and healers.

Not only does this book feature some beautiful animals, but connected to these souls are some amazing Guardians who want the very best for their animals. They have shown incredible courage and love, and for the sake of their animals they have been prepared to walk down an unfamiliar path, and consider notions which may seem crazy to a lot of people. But in having the courage to embrace them, they have not only deepened the connections to their animals, but they have transformed their own lives in the process.

I hope in reading about them that it will give you the courage too to follow some of the ideas in the book, and consider ways of relating/being with your animal that you may never have previously considered. We all have it within us to do this work. By doing so, we can make the changes the world requires. It needs all of us to come together and awaken to our divinity. This will allow the creation of a more loving and peaceful world, where not only we can thrive, but the animals can too.

As you have picked this book up, then you are clearly open and prepared to perceiving animals in a much deeper way. Hopefully, if you don't already, this book will encourage you to see them as soulful Beings. When you recognise the soul in another, then you will also see it in yourself. Life becomes so much more magical when you change the lens through which you see.

So what is my wish for you the reader? I hope this book encourages you to walk a soulful path with the animals, and I hope it gives you the courage to travel on your own amazing journey. If we are to create a better future, or any future at all on this beautiful planet, then we all need to wake up to our responsibilities and our connectedness to every living being. Together we can move mountains. All it needs is love – the most powerful force in the Universe. Our beloved animals have this in shedloads. They are the ones who can show us the way!

THE AWAKENING

I always say that it only takes one miracle in life to change your way of thinking. Once you have experienced something so great, so profound and so extraordinarily impossible, then you can never again return to your old way of thinking. You are forever changed, and it is for one simple reason: you have experienced something that was real but was beyond our physical laws of science. And if one "impossible" thing can occur, then doesn't it completely dismantle the idea that we live in a material, physical and logical world contained within our five senses? It also opens you up to the idea that absolutely anything is possible. It is no wonder that such a change in thinking is termed "an awakening." For yes, we are waking up from the illusions of the world.

My awakening happened in the spring of 2012. In the years since, my perception of the world has changed so dramatically, and I have worked so hard on my spiritual development that I barely recognise the person I once was. Simply put, I am no longer that person!

Even though I have told my awakening story in my previous two books, it is appropriate to tell it here also, because this is where my journey started. It was from here that everything else followed. These events have been the bedrock of my belief system, and they are the foundational blocks for everything that follows. Whenever any doubts break into my awareness (and let's face it, all of us, however strong our belief systems, do suffer periods of doubt and do question from time to time whether it is just our mind making it all up), I always resurrect the memories surrounding the events of March 2012. In doing so, my faith is instantly restored.

This time around, I am telling my story in much greater depth and detail, and I hope that even if you have read it before, you will perhaps take something else away from it this time around. Maybe it will touch you even more profoundly and deeply than it did previously. Certainly in the re-telling, I seem to gain greater insights each time.

It is no surprise, considering the nature of this book, that my awakening was very much connected to an animal. Not just any animal, but one with whom I had shared 26 years of my life. It was this horse who was to open me up to a much deeper way of perceiving animals, helping me to recognise that just like us, they do possess a soul. More importantly, I was to learn the great gifts such animals hold for us. I now have no doubt whatsoever that most animals who come into our lives are here to teach, pass on lessons, and help us to grow. In short, they are here to help evolve our very souls.

I really hope that my story helps any of you dealing with grief. The sadness of losing someone you love, whether a human or animal, can be all consuming and soul destroying. But knowing that even in the deepest moments of grief that there are treasures to be unearthed, can really help us to face up to the dark times. Although it sounds harsh, the lesson I learned was that sadness and grief are a choice. When we choose to see it in a different way, then the sadness just melts away, and can even be replaced with joy. It sounds impossible, but if it can happen to me, it can happen to anyone.

My story starts with an extraordinary horse who entered my life in the summer when I was twenty-one.

MY EXTRAORDINARY HORSE

From the very first day that Tiffany came into my life, it was a union of souls. We just adored each other! She was the horse I had always dreamed of owning, and I must have felt good to her too, because from the very first day of being with me, she was whinnying and galloping up to me in the field whenever I called her.

The next 26 years passed in a blur of complete joy with this amazing horse. We literally had a ball! I believe that all horses have lessons for us, and this horse seemed to have been sent to teach me about the joyful bond that is possible between human and horse.

My twenties were a difficult time for me, but my horse always knew how to pick me up. Nothing was out of bounds for us. We had complete trust and faith in each other, and those years were a time of exploring all the wonderful horse activities that were available, including days out, where we would picnic in beautiful countryside, creating make shift cross-country jumps in the woods. When I was with my horse, life was perfect!

In many ways, Tiffany was quite extraordinary. She never tired, and even in her thirties her energy had still not abated. No other horse on the yard could keep up with her fast walk. She loved being ridden as much as I loved riding her. But despite her incredibly high energy, she never, ever used it against me. I don't remember a single time when she bucked, reared or bolted. She was incredibly kind and sweet, and took the very best care of me. I was humbled by her desire to please me and make me happy.

As well as her high energy, she also had extraordinary telepathic abilities. If we were going on a short ride, she would jog from the start. If it was a long ride, she would walk, realising she needed to save her energy. She always knew!

If I was hurting in some way (be it physical or emotional) she would pick up on it, and would try and comfort or accommodate me however she could. One winter, I had torn muscles in my neck and shoulders and was struggling to lift her headcollar and bridle. Not a problem with Tiffany around! She would just put her head very close to the ground, making it easy for me. Nothing was ever too much trouble. She really was my perfect horse!

We rode together until she was 34. At that age she was still enjoying her riding, and her energy was still very high, but she had started to feel a little unsound in trot, due to having arthritis in her back fetlock joint. The time had come to retire her.

Three weeks into her retirement, Tiffany appeared very well indeed. She would gallop around crazily when I went to fetch her in, and would canter in sideways as I led her down the track to her stable. Dancing and prancing was all this horse ever knew, and I instinctively felt that she would never have signed up to a long, drawn-out illness. The feeling was growing within me that we didn't have long left together in the physical world. There was nothing in my horse's behaviour that was indicative that she would be leaving any time soon, but I couldn't shake the feeling.

My horse, who had gifted me so much in life, had saved the best until last. For what was to unfold in the following days would change my life forever.

The Dream

Throughout my life, dreams have been quite significant. They have taught me things and I easily understand the symbolic messages that are so often conveyed to me. On the odd occasion, I have also received premonitions. But the dream I had in March 2012 was very strange indeed, and unlike anything I had experienced before or since.

On awakening, the details of the dream eluded me. However, I was very much aware that I had spent the night with my horse, but on a soul level rather than the physical. There was a sense that the dream had lasted a long time, and there was a recollection of our souls merging and being in total harmony; like we knew and understood each other at a very deep level. I was left with the feeling of being touched by the essence of something beautiful and other worldly. My soul felt soothed and peaceful.

I felt so affected by it that I mentioned it to my husband. A brave move! My husband is not in the least bit spiritual and his version of reality does not extend beyond his five senses. His reaction was very much as expected - I was just completely potty!

Still in a daze from the dream, I went downstairs to make breakfast and turned the computer on. I discovered the next beautiful thing to happen that morning: an Animal Communication (my first), had been carried out on Tiffany and was sitting in my inbox. It was meant to have been completed a few weeks earlier, but through some strange twist, it had disappeared off the communicators list so had been delayed until now. Today was clearly the day I was supposed to receive it, and with the events that were to follow, it was destined to become a parting gift.

I was blown away – it was a wonderful testimony to our bond and adventures over the years, and it was completely accurate. The communicator had picked up on all the things which were unique to Tiffany: her incredible energy, her good health, the very long, joyful and amazing bond we had shared, the adventures we had undertaken, and most importantly my horse's big heart. Tiffany had actually told her that, *"She had tried her hardest for me."* The horse that she described was without doubt my special, unique horse!

Before I even ventured up the yard that morning, everything seemed surreal. In hindsight, I should have been more prepared for the events which were to unfold, for I was being given a warning; one I refused to pay any heed to. In just a couple of short hours, my heart would be shattered. The time had come to say goodbye!

The Last Goodbye

Arriving at the stables that morning, there was nothing to give me cause for concern. Tiffany greeted me with her usual whinny and ate her feed with her normal enthusiasm. It was just a typical day, or so I thought…

It was only as we neared the field that I realised something was badly wrong. Tiffany was finding it hard to walk straight and her quarters were starting to wobble from side to side. I called the vet immediately. The dream from the night before began to haunt me. Was it her way of saying goodbye?

In the last hour of her life, as we were waiting for the vet to arrive, I was very conscious of the fact that here was a horse who understood exactly what was happening to her. She seemed to have a lucidity about her that was beyond normal animal understanding. In the huge neighs she gave to her horse best friend and then to myself, it was obvious she was saying goodbye.

At one point, she made it very clear to me that she didn't want me to leave her. I was going to walk back to the yard to let people know what was unfolding, but Tiffany kept nickering to me. With her head over my shoulder, she was pulling me back. *"Please don't leave me"* she was beseeching. How could I refuse my horse's last request?

As I waited for the vet to arrive, I stayed in the field with my horse. She stood in front of me, her head resting on my shoulder, but every few minutes she would walk in small circles, whinnying at the same time. It was not a distressed or pained sound – it was her happy, greeting whinny. I was immediately reminded of my Nan a couple of years earlier. Hours before she passed away, she talked about a little boy and girl standing by her bed. Intuitively, I now felt that Tiffany's mum had come for her, and I was saying goodbye. My heart broke at this point and the tears fell – there was no doubt in my mind that I was saying goodbye to my beloved and special horse.

This pattern of behaviour continued right up until the vet walked up the path towards us, about an hour later. As she did so, Tiffany started circling all the way up the field, collapsing near the gate. She had held on long enough and now it was time to go. As my horse breathed her last, I lay down with her, my arms wrapped around her neck. In between my gasping sobs, I thanked her for everything she had done for me and for being the most amazing and wonderful horse it was possible to be. Like the brilliant and dazzling star on her head, this horse had lit my path for the last 26 years. That light had now been snuffed out. How on earth would I live my life without her? My soul mate had gone.

The Sunflower

The rest of the day passed in a haze of misery. I cried until there were no tears left. In between my sobs, I prayed and pleaded, *"Please give me a sign that my horse is in a good place. Tiffany if you can hear me, please let me know you are happy and at peace."* I prayed over and over, knowing that only a sign would comfort me.

The next day, a Saturday, I was determined to keep my promise to a friend. She had gone away for the weekend, and I was to look after and exercise her horse. We set out on our ride - me on my friend's horse, and my daughter and her friend (both aged 13) on their ponies.

As we headed home along a well-used bridlepath, we witnessed something very unusual. There was a single sunflower situated right on the edge of the path. Typically it had a large head, but it wasn't on the usual thin, long stem. This one had a thick, short stem, about 1 ½ feet in length. Not only that, but it was absolutely perfect. There wasn't a mark or flaw on it!

The next day it was there again. This time we were riding the opposite way, and it seemed even more remarkable. Situated on its own, part of the way up a gradual incline, we could see it from a fair distance away. It looked surreal! The thought entered my head that perhaps it was artificial, but as we rode past, there was no mistaking the stem entering the ground. As with the day before, I just kept repeating, *"Wow, I haven't seen a sunflower that perfect before, and on such a short stem, or on a bridlepath."* At that moment I would have loved for one of us to have had a camera mode on our cheap phones.

An hour later when we rode back, the sunflower had gone. Disappeared! As my daughter exclaimed her shock, my dazed and fuzzy brain started to kick into gear. This was the 11th of March in the UK, not August which is the normal time for sunflowers. Nightly temperatures had touched as low as -5 the week before. It was absolutely impossible!

A memory was stirring of something I had read: that when our loved ones transition, they try to send signs they are well. These signs are often in the form of flowers which bloom out of season. The fact this sunflower had just "disappeared" made it even more significant. There was no denying it, this was my sign!

Just looking at a sunflower has always made me feel happy and uplifted. So the message I was receiving seemed very clear indeed. There could be no better sign telling me that my horse was residing in a beautiful and magical place. She was happy and sending her love! It brought me so much peace to know that.

As time passed, I began to see an even deeper meaning in the sunflower. As the head turns towards the sun for light and sustenance, I was being encouraged to do the same. There is no denying that witnessing this sunflower was pivotal in my spiritual journey. For if something can appear and disappear so easily, then what does it say about our physical laws? Are they as real as we perceive them to be? Doesn't it just prove that absolutely anything is possible? Like the sunflower, I would turn to face the light. My search for a different truth would take me on a life changing journey.

But before that, another miracle was beckoning! I was about to receive the deepest, most profound healing of my life.

The Healing

Although the sunflower had given me the proof I needed that my horse was residing in a wonderful place, I still grieved horribly, and I was still crying over my breakfast. The thought of not seeing her beautiful face every day was making my heart ache.

The fourth morning after her death brought added distress. I was to turn out my friend's two horses and their stables were right next to Tiffany's. How could I bear to hear them neigh to me, and for Tiff's neigh to be absent?

Pulling myself together, I dragged myself up the yard. But there was a huge surprise in store! Instead of the usual greeting, I was met by silence. For the first time ever these horses did not acknowledge me. How did they know that their silence was so needed that morning?

Gratefully, I opened Esther's door and went in to change her rug. The beautiful thoroughbred in the adjoining stable put his head over the wall. As I offered him my hand, I expected his normal retreat to the back of the stable. But not today! Instead, he started kissing and licking me on the side of my neck. Amazed, I told him how wonderful that felt. My praise intensified his action.

At one point he stopped, standing in front of me, his large liquid eyes staring directly into mine. That was when I noticed it. Water had started to form in one eye, and very slowly a trickle ran down his beautiful dark face. I watched in disbelief. This just wasn't possible. Horses can't cry. But there was no mistaking it. An idea formed in my mind, but I could barely entertain it. This horse had lost his field mate 6 months before. He understood the pain of loss. So was he now empathising with my loss, comforting me in the best way he knew how?

As my mind grappled with this unbelievable notion, Esther suddenly started to take an interest in Monty's actions. She looked at him bemused with a *"What on Earth are you doing?"* expression on her face. Then, amazingly, she started copying his kissing and licking on the other side of my neck.

Bliss! For about ten minutes, I was taken somewhere otherworldly; a place where man and horse are completely unified in compassion, empathy and understanding. It was a language of pure love; a meeting of hearts, and no words were necessary. For me, it was also a place where joy and gratitude started to surface from deep within me. For now I was witness to a great truth. This was a truth I had suppressed for a very long time, for fear of being ridiculed. Instead, I had handed my soul over to a conditioning society, and conceded to the common belief that a horse is an animal who can't reason and empathise like a human. Now this lie was staring me in the face. At that moment, I felt humbled by these wonderful souls, and I felt sadness that they were so greatly misunderstood.

A sense of purpose was arising from deep within me, growing in intensity until I knew for certain what I had to do. My promise to the horses was made. I had encountered a revelation from which there was no turning back. The rest of my life would be devoted to helping these beautiful souls be better understood. How, I didn't know, but help them I must. For when you have uncovered a valuable treasure, you can't then bury it again, pretending it didn't exist.

Our connection was broken by a human voice shouting, *"Hello!"* We all jumped apart, like we had been caught doing something we shouldn't. The spell was broken!

As I walked out of the stable that day, another realisation dawned. The horses hadn't just felt my pain and responded to it, they had gifted me the deepest and most profound healing of my life. As I walked into the light of the yard, my whole being seemed to fill with that light. Every part of me was consumed by the most incredible feeling of joy and happiness.

It was like I had been touched by the divine, and through those horses I still believe to this day that I had. All my pain had just vanished. Instead, I felt immense joy and gratitude for having spent 26 years with the most wonderful horse imaginable. It was like my horse had died ten years previously, and I had completely come to terms with it, recognising not only the huge gifts she had brought into my life, but appreciating the fact that she had not had to endure a long or debilitating illness. Her transition had been quick and painless, and I had been granted the gift of being with her throughout. Now, I just felt immense awe and appreciation for everything that had transpired.

That day was the most transformative day of my life. It was the day my life changed forever. A new path had opened up in front of me and I was determined to walk down it. Little did I know then how magical this path would be! In time, I would learn that my horse had left an unbelievable legacy!

Tiffany's Legacy

The events surrounding Tiffany's transition had left me shaken and stirred. Everything I thought I understood about reality had been dismantled in front of my eyes. As I started to fit new pieces together, I was creating an altogether different picture. This new reality I was building would bring me much greater peace, joy and happiness.

A new horse came into my life; a very different horse to Tiffany, but a horse with many lessons to teach me. Tiffany had opened up a new path for me, but it was Jazz who very much led me down it. There was no coincidence in the fact that she turned up at this stage of my journey, when I so badly needed a spiritual mentor. She took on this role perfectly, teaching me way more than I taught her. I learned that animals too have destinies they wish to fulfil, and this horse made it very clear that she wanted to partner me in a healer capacity. Part of her role was to channel a book through me, which I self-published (*A Horse's Voice*, released in 2023). This process was so magical – again I can barely get my head around it!

A big part of my ensuing journey was to learn and practise Animal Communication and become attuned to Reiki (Master level), in addition to working hard on removing my conditioned thinking and limiting beliefs. Some things really surprised me! Not for one second would I have ever envisaged writing a book. Having barely written anything since I had left school, other than work letters, I did not consider myself a writer in any shape or form. Yet writing was what I was encouraged to do, and five years after Tiffany's transition, I self-published a book (*Seeker of the Light,* published in 2017), detailing all the amazing things that had happened to me, and setting these out in a framework of spiritual beliefs. Needless to say, I very much felt like I was just a channel, as the book seemed to write itself.

Behind all these blessings lies a very special horse whose love is eternal. If it wasn't for her, I wouldn't be where I am today. Her spirit and her essence are still very much alive and working through me, helping to motivate me in my desire to help horses and all animals be better understood.

As I started this story, so I end. My darkest day turned out to be one of the most transformational of my life, containing so many gifts and blessings. Now with my eyes open, I can appreciate the beauty in things which I had previously taken for granted.

But more importantly, my eyes had been well and truly opened to the true nature of animals, and just how deeply those connections are weaved into our soul. It was inevitable that my search for answers would take me deep into the field of Animal Communication and energy healing. What I was to discover in the resulting years would bring me great peace and happiness. My mission was born!

My horse whose shining light had guided me for all those years, had saved the best until last. She has gifted me a magical legacy!

PART 1 – ANIMALS AS TEACHERS

*"When I look into the eyes of a dog
I could cry at the love staring back at me.
This is the love we need to harness
To have any chance of saving the world."*

I don't know about you, but I have always felt so out of place in this world; like an alien that has landed in a crazy world; one that makes no sense whatsoever.

It is my belief that this feeling is more common than I used to think, and that many of us feel this way at some point. When you think about it, our world with its emphasis on separation, materialism and the logical mind is very conflicted with who we truly are, which is Spirits having a human experience. Western society has diverted our gaze in completely the wrong direction. Is it any wonder that many of us feel like strangers in a strange world? In a world where minds are given supremacy over hearts, many people, particularly those who are sensitive, compassionate and empathic, are going to struggle.

I believe that this is why so many of us are drawn to animals. All the spiritual people I know seem to have a very deep love for animals, recognizing that here are Beings who have never forgotten who they are, and who have retained their connection to the natural world. Us on the other hand, through our ignorance in believing that we were superior to the rest of creation, decided to separate from it and go it alone. Looking at the state of the world now, makes you realise how misaligned our thinking was, beguiled by greed and notions of our own self-importance.

But animals have come to our rescue, doing what they have always done; being there for us in our hour of need and leading us back into our hearts and souls. As they lead us back to our true selves, we can once again connect back to our love centre.

In this section of the book, I focus on three animals who had very valuable teachings for me. One of these is my own horse Jazz, who really has been a master teacher. I could probably have devoted a whole book to her story. Needless to say, hers is a very large chapter. One of her really big lessons was to demonstrate that animals too have soul purpose for being here.

Harry's story is powerful because it highlights the sensitivity of some animals to things we would never tolerate for ourselves. So should we be asking this of our animals? At the very least, it is important to feel empathy for their situation, and then support them in the best way we can. For Harry, reiki offered huge support, giving him what he needed to step into his power.

Animals can teach us a lot about joy, and Silver had some very powerful lessons for me in the art of joy. Despite his being a chapter devoted to joy, you may need some tissues handy for the end of the story. You have been warned!

The animals in this section of the book were also instrumental in directing me towards Animal Communication/Reiki healing as a profession. For someone who has always suffered from low self-esteem, these animals, through their transformation and lessons, really helped me recognise the massive value in the work I was doing, and they helped boost my confidence. I started to see that these practices were more than just a bit of fun; they actually hold huge value for the animals, their Guardians, and for the communicator, leaving all of us profoundly touched and forever changed by these interactions.

JAZZ

A Lesson in Soul Purpose

"The soul of an animal is untouched by the ego which is prevalent in Man.
Many domestic animals who live alongside us Humans
Choose to live a life of unselfish endeavour.
To be man's friend, teacher and saviour.
When you allow them to live out their soul purpose
Then you receive a blessing which is second to none."

My horse Jazz entered my life in the summer of 2012. She has been a powerful teacher, and it is no coincidence that she came to me when she did, at the start of my spiritual journey. There are many lessons that she has graced my life with and I feel privileged to have learned so much from her. It is for this reason that the chapter is so long. It was hard to know where to stop, such has been the enormity of her teachings.

Soul Purpose

Sadly, I have to confess that it had never entered my awareness that animal's may have a soul purpose in coming to Earth. Jazz was to deliver me a very powerful lesson regarding this!

As she stood on the horsebox, having just arrived on our yard, she turned to stare at me. It was like a bolt of electricity just surged through my body, for there was no mistaking the ancient wisdom staring back at me. In that moment, I knew that Jazz was going to be a horse like no other.

Like anyone who takes on a new horse, I had ideas and dreams as to what we would do together. My plans involved hacking, competing in some low level show-jumping, joining a riding club, and I also hoped that Lauren would eventually be able to ride and compete her.

Well, what do they say about best laid plans? What transpired proved to be far more fulfilling than anything my ego mind could conjure up.

It was clear very early on that Jazz had entered my life to tame my ego tendencies. By overcoming the ego mind, I would further my journey down the spiritual path, because it is reckoned that the path to enlightenment is very much a journey in overcoming the ego. I can certainly vouch for it being a much more fulfilling, peaceful and happier life, when you start to listen to the quieter soul mind, as opposed to the loud, negative ego mind.

So those early attempts to improve my horse's agility and suppleness, were thrown back in my face. *"Why are you attempting to fix me?"* I could hear my horse say. *"I accept you for who you are, so why can't you accept me for who I am?"* Yes, she did have a point. We spend so much time trying to improve our animals (particularly our horses), yet they just have total acceptance for the person who turns up for them every day. They may try and train us, but this is completely different.

Then came the revelation that Jazz had something much greater up her sleeve, than being a riding horse. As I led her down to the menage one day, there was no mistaking the voice in my head as being hers. *"This is all wrong"* she protested, *"I came into your life to lead you away from riding. We are to form a healing partnership together."* Well, there was nothing like that statement to stop me dead in my tracks. I knew I needed to explore this further.

A lady who writes for a spiritual magazine read Jazz's aura, and confirmed that she had a beautiful rainbow aura; a sign of spiritual advancement. She mentioned that she was no ordinary horse, and didn't want to be seen as one. So this was one validation of Jazz's spiritual energy.

Then, my reiki teacher came out and astounded me by announcing that Jazz wanted to co-write a book with me. It sounded absolutely bonkers, but so much had happened to me by then, that I just put my faith in it and decided to give it a go; and boy, I was not disappointed.

The book that flowed through me as I sat in Jazz's stable was to me nothing short of miraculous. Consciously, I had no idea what I was going to write. I had deliberately not tried to think about it, because I just wanted it to flow through like Animal Communication. That way, with my mind completely blank and turned off, I would know that what was coming through me was not my own voice. And that was how my second book, *"A Horse's Voice"* was born.

It wasn't just the fact that I was a vessel for the book to flow through, but it was also the change in Jazz's energy and mood which convinced me that my horse really was instrumental in this book's creation. From the moment I sat with her and put my pen on the paper, all traces of grumpiness just vanished. Up until then, Jazz would snap at me like a crocodile if I attempted to put the bit in her mouth, and she would pin her ears back and try and bite if you came near her with the saddle. She was also planting in the menage and refusing to move. But all those traits disappeared once we started writing. I had explained to her that she still needed to be ridden, for it was good for her agility and suppleness, so even though our routine didn't change at all, she was without doubt a very different horse. It was this change in her personality which convinced my skeptical, scientific daughter that this was all for real.

This was quite an amazing revelation for me. For now, I recognized that animals too have aims and ambitions they want to fulfil which are very much tied up with their soul purpose for coming to Earth. And in working towards them, just like us, it can make them much happier and more fulfilled.

Healing abilities

It wasn't just writing the book; Jazz was revealing her spiritual qualities in other ways. Her empathy and concern for Silver, her field mate, was covered in the book, *"A Horse's Voice"*, so I won't repeat the stories here.

On another two separate occasions, Jazz had acted like a conduit for healing.

A friend who I had become reunited with after about 25 years apart, had come up the yard to meet Jazz. She walked into her stable and her hands started shaking quite noticeably. Intuitively, she felt she needed to place her vibrating hands onto Jazz's head. As she did so, Jazz closed her eyes completely and appeared to be in a trance. A few minutes later, it became apparent that my friend was having a deeply emotive experience. She started thanking Jazz over and over again, as the tears coursed down her cheeks. She explained to me that Jazz had been passing messages to her relating to her horse, who had transitioned five years before, telling her she was safe and happy, and it was time for her to move on. Not only that, but my friend reported feeling an incredible sense of peace and love. The next day, she reported having had the best night's sleep in a very long time.

Then, two weeks later, a similar thing happened with another friend, who had asked if she could come up and practise her Reiki on Jazz. Immediately, things weren't going to plan. On asking permission from Jazz to carry out Reiki, conveyed through her pendulum, she was receiving a definite no. My pendulum indicated the same. As my friend stood there shocked and crushed, I remembered what had happened two weeks previously, and I suggested that maybe Jazz wanted to give her some Reiki. As my friend asked the question, her pendulum swung out like never before. The answer was a definite yes. My friend entered a meditative state and put her hands on Jazz's withers. Twenty minutes later, my friend recounted her experience. She had entered a very deep trance indeed, where she had been nearly falling into Jazz, and in that state she had been receiving messages pertaining to her dog, as well as very deep feelings of peace and love. She left the yard in a state of bliss, reporting that she felt slightly drunk. Weeks later, my friend reported that the deep feelings of peace and tranquillity had stayed with her.

These events have helped me realise that animals are natural healers; to such an extent, that I consider Reiki a shared experience, where we can both enjoy the energy as equals, allowing healing to go where it is needed.

Reading energy

I have always been fascinated by how easily Jazz can read another horse's energy and character. This emotional intelligence seems to far exceed our own. For example, when we moved her to a new yard, we put a small pony in the field with her. Jazz was delighted with the idea of sharing her field and came trotting over, neighing her head off, but when she was about ten feet away, she stopped dead and moved to the side. Very correctly, she had picked up that this pony was shy (she had previously been bullied by another horse) and she needed her space. Jazz completely recognized this and was determined not to crowd her. They started grazing about ten feet away from each other, and Jazz gradually drew closer, until they were nose to nose. That was precisely the way to win around a new friend.

Another incident was even more intriguing. There was a horse on the yard who had been abused in her early life, and, although she adored her Guardian, she was not so keen on other people. Her stable was about thirty feet away from Jazz's on the opposite side, and while I was waiting for Jazz to finish her tea, I was talking to the lady of this horse. Jazz finished her tea, and she was showing very clear signs that she didn't like me being too close to this horse. If I moved towards the horse, Jazz would start neighing and throwing her head up and down, as if to say, *"Don't step any closer."* The moment I stepped back, she would relax. I did this a few times, and there was no mistaking Jazz's concern. The lady I was talking to also didn't fail to notice it and she too was astonished.

This also shows how horses are aware of each other's personalities, even when they are not kept near each other. Their stables were not close to each other, and their fields were even further away, and yet Jazz seemed very much aware of this horse's distrust and aggression directed towards other people. I have always believed that horses have much more awareness of each other than we have ever credited them with, and this incident just goes to prove it.

As well as reading the energy from other horses, Jazz is also very attuned to the energy of people around her. She adores young children, and she is also very attentive to any person who is upset.

But there was one incident which just amazed me. Not just because she was able to read this person's energy the moment she encountered him, but she also seemed to sense what was going to happen. This is the closest thing I have witnessed of a horse having a premonition. I wrote about the event as soon as it happened and I am recounting it here.

The Dentist

My horse knew. I am sure of it. Walking towards her field, headcollar in hand, she did something she had never done before in the previous nine years she had been with me. She had been standing quietly by her gate until she spotted me. Then, it was like someone had flicked a switch. Up and down the field she thundered, like a streak of light, reaching speeds I didn't know she was capable of, the whole time neighing and screaming "Save me, save me." But from what? I was soon to discover.

I stood quietly, eyes lowered. A few times she sailed past me, snorting like a stallion. Eventually, she responded to the calm, loving energy I directed her way. Her head dropped, followed by her adrenaline. I quietly placed on her headcollar, and she walked softly by my side for the few minutes it took to reach the barn.

In her stable, I gave her a little Reiki, asking her to please trust me. With soft eyes and relaxed body, she was enjoying the beautiful shared energy. Everything was good in her world.

I talked softly to her, explaining what was about to happen. Her eye settled on me, and I knew she was listening. The plan was to lead her into the stable at the end of the row, where her teeth would be attended to.

Dentistry, like shoeing, had never been an issue for Jazz. She had always been relaxed, calm and accommodating, knowing that these people were trying to help her. But this occasion was a bit different. We would be dealing with a new dentist on the yard, one that had come highly recommended. So much so that 14 horses on the yard had been booked in with him. Jazz was the last to go.

Jazz walked calmly into the stable, placing her trust in my instructions. But as she turned around to face the dentist, she was met with what I can only describe as hostile energy. This man had adopted a predator stance – standing tall, muscles rigid, giving my horse the hard stare. It was obvious to me that my beautiful thoroughbred, so sensitive to energy, instantly felt threatened. Her head shot up and I could see the whites of her eyes. OMG! What had I done?

The next half hour was very difficult to witness. Yes, it could have been a lot worse, and most people would probably perceive it a small price to pay for what was supposedly good dentistry work. But I am not "most people." There was no shouting or smacking (unless you count the thumps on the shoulder), but this man's energy was screaming at my horse "You had better behave or else." He was rude and disrespectful to my horse, calling her a "cow" and reducing her to an "It." She was stripped of her sentience, her soul and her dignity. My beautiful horse's muscles were held rigid in terror, and she was trembling so hard that she was rendered a quivering wreck.

So where was I in all this? Forced to stand in the doorway, lest my horse decided to explode when she came out of her "freeze" state, I was not even able to reassure her with a comforting touch. "Too dangerous a situation" I was told, "Just leave her with me." This was not a request, but an order. But for crying out loud, this is my beloved horse with whom I have spent the last nine years. I trust her not to hurt me a thousand times more than this man in front of me.

I am ashamed to admit it, but I was not there for my horse. As an empath, I was mirroring the same shut down state as Jazz. Silent, rigid and locked inside my body, unable to move or speak! I could feel the sympathy of the people standing behind me, but I could also hear their thoughts. "There is no need to be so sensitive. He is only doing his job after all. So what if he has to put a bit of pressure on the horse."

Finally, it was at an end. I was handed her rope and told to be very careful leading her out of the stable as she would probably run out. But this part of the story I did have control over. As I felt my horse relax at the feel of my touch, I sent her a wave of love, calm and softness from my heart to hers, along with a picture of walking calmly out of the stable. Very, very slowly, as if in slow motion we stepped out, sauntering down the rows of stables. Would anyone notice this softness, this calm? Probably not! People only see what they want to.

It was my horse who needed comforting, but she was the one there for me. As I led her to her field, she covered my face with soft, gentle kisses. "It is not your fault. You weren't to know" she was saying. Later, when I went to her field, she embraced me with a huge whinny, walking over to greet me.

The rest of the evening she was so attentive, so loving. We put our horses through so much, yet they are always there for us, beseeching us to let go of our grievances and to live *in the moment. Forgiving us for everything we put them through.*

Just to put you, the reader's mind, at rest, Jazz's teeth are now attended to by a man who used to be a vet and is now qualified as a dentist. She always loved the quiet, gentle energy of this skilled man, and even after her bad experience with the other dentist, she just accepted having her teeth done with her usual, calm acceptance.

It has really made me realise how careful we need to be regarding the people who handle our horses. Respect, empathy and compassion should be taught as part of the training of professional equine services. I know there are times when a firmer hand is needed, but this can still be given in a respectful way.

The benefits of Animal Communication (AC)

It is often said that with Animal Communication, it is much harder to hear your own animals than it is with those you know nothing about.

To a certain degree this is true. With AC, you do have to be very careful that you keep your thinking mind out of it, because as soon as this takes over, then you are not experiencing a direct communication with the animal. It is just the mind creating the story. It is easier in some ways communicating with an animal you know nothing about because then whatever flows through is more likely to be genuine rather than the mind filling in the gaps.

Nevertheless, I do think you can learn to communicate with your own animal, and this can be of huge benefit to both of you. It is just important to keep the thinking mind out of the way, and to let things flow through. I give examples below of some of the things that Jazz has told me in the past, which enabled me to create the changes she needed. I have tried to pick examples where I know that my thinking mind played no part in what came through.

On one yard, in the summer, all of the horses were coming in during the day and were turned out late afternoon/evening time. I was starting to notice with Jazz that she was a bit reluctant to head out to her field, and on one particular day, with her ears pinned back flat against her head and her tendency to keep stopping, she was being decidedly grumpy about it.

"What on Earth is the matter?" I asked her, having no idea why she was reacting so vehemently. Immediately I heard her say *"I am hungry and you don't put any hay out in my field. I only get hay when I come into the stable."*

"But that's because you have lots of grass in your field" I pointed out.

"Yes, but I don't like that grass" she retorted. *"Can you please put out some hay."*

Well don't ever accuse me of not listening to my horse. I went back to the stables, put a pile out with her, and blow me down, there wasn't a blade of hay left the next day. From then on, hay was put out every night. My horse returned to her willing self and the problem was resolved. As the weeks went by, it became very clear that Jazz only liked eating the grass towards the bottom of the field. The rest of her fairly large field resembled a jungle by the time we left the yard.

Clearly, it was only Jazz who had the problem with the grass not being to her liking, because the two horses who were grazed in the field after we left had shortened the grass in next to no time. Guess I have a horse with delectable tastes!

It isn't many times that I hear Jazz's voice when I am with her. A lot of the time, I have to wait until I get home, go into a light trance and tune into her telepathically; but there have been a few times when I could hear her directly.

Another such time was when my daughter was riding her. We were very fortunate with the yard we were on, because there were three arenas to ride in. One of them was a large jumping arena, and it had just been resurfaced. The day we took Jazz in there, the surface looked immaculate and the jumps were well laid out.

Jazz had always enjoyed her jumping and was never less than enthusiastic about it, but on this occasion, after jumping a few of the fences, she had planted her feet and was refusing to move.

"Can you please ask her what is wrong?" Lauren asked me, to my great delight. I just love it when my scientific vet of a daughter asks me to do my thing.

Her reply made us look around the arena in astonishment. *"The ground is terribly uneven and I don't feel safe"* she had said. *"Can't you see how deep it is in places? I feel like I am going to lose my footing."*

Sure enough, on a careful examination, we could see that she was indeed right. The sand was deep in parts, there was no denying it. We immediately took her out of there. A few days later she attended a jumping clinic in another arena, demonstrating her normal enthusiasm.

A couple of months later, after a few horses had fallen, it was decided that a lot more money needed to be spent, and the jumping arena was kitted out with a much safer surface. We never had any further problems in there.

It is so important to listen to what your horse is telling you, because it really can be saving them from serious injury. When our horses say no to our instructions, there is always a valid reason for it which needs exploring.

In many ways, Jazz has made it easy for us because she so clearly tells us when something is wrong, but many horses will just try and comply with everything that is asked of them, and this can be very damaging for them. It is good to demonstrate to your horse that you are listening and acting on what they tell you.

About a year after the above incident, Lauren was jumping at a show. Jazz hadn't seemed quite right in the first class, but she had still gone clear and been placed. Then, as she was warming up for the second class, it quickly became apparent that something clearly wasn't right. For the first time ever, Jazz refused a fence. The woman in the collecting ring thought we were over-reacting when we asked for her to be withdrawn from the competition, but we absolutely knew something wasn't right with her. Jazz backed up our decision by completely refusing to take even one step towards a pole on the ground. It is times like this when I just love having a sassy horse who will stand up for herself and make her opinions felt. The woman had no choice but to comply and withdraw them from the competition.

This was a time when I couldn't immediately hear what Jazz wanted to say about the problem. When I arrived home, I tuned into her and she immediately enabled me to feel painful shoulders, caused by the saddle slipping forwards. And the reason? Lauren had been riding her in a new sheepskin girth, and it was clearly causing the saddle to move forwards. Not noticeable to us, but clearly felt by Jazz.

A week later, with her old girth back in place, Jazz was back to jumping well again and in the jumping clinic they were partaking in, she jumped the highest jump ever. Well, when the tack is right, the horse can perform their best.

Enabling an animal to let you feel their physical pain is one of the easiest things to do, and particularly with horses where incorrectly fitting tack can cause pain, it is a very useful thing to be able to do.

Sometimes the speed in which you can resolve a problem when you know what is going on can be phenomenal. Lauren had been doing some flatwork with Jazz, and it was immediately clear that she was not moving into canter properly. She was running into it rather than effortlessly gliding into it.

Sensing there was a physical problem, when I arrived home, I tuned into Jazz to see what she could show me. I immediately felt some back pain, and I was given a very clear impression that the saddle was lying too close to her spine and needed re-stuffing.

Sure enough, when we went back up the yard on the evening, and we took away the numnah (pad between the back and saddle), it was very clear that yes, it was too close to the spine. Fortunately, someone on the yard was having a saddle fitter to her horse the very next day, so she was able to re-stuff the saddle for us. The canter problem was immediately resolved.

Sometimes, when you ask your animal to show you something, it is immediately clear what they are telling you. You really don't need any AC skills, but to just be open to what they are showing you. Our animals are communicating all the time and we just need to join the dots to what they are saying.

In the summer of 2021, I felt that Jazz was not really happy. I went to her field, and I asked her why she wasn't happy and what she needed. Immediately, she asked me to scratch her. Now this was unusual, because even though she has always liked being scratched on her withers, she had never before asked me to do this. As I rubbed, with her showing clear enjoyment, there was no escaping the words searing through my head. *"I need another horse to be able to do this with."*

Sadly, I knew that I had to face up to the truth. Even though she had horses on both sides of her, the rustic fencing with the wire running along the top made it nigh impossible for any horse grooming to be carried out. She was lonely and needed a field mate.

We had bought a horse for Lauren eight months before, but we had to keep her on a separate yard because there was no room at the one Jazz was on. Now, I realised that it was of the utmost importance to get Jazz and Rosie together, and I had to face the fact that it may be years before a space became available on Jazz's yard. The only alternative was to see if a space would come up on Rosie's yard, or to move them both to an entirely new yard.

I explained this to Jazz, but I know she didn't believe me. She can see straight through to my soul, and she knows that I am a terrible procrastinator. But I did mean it, and my intention was that I would start looking as soon as we returned from our holiday, which we were due to take in a week's time.

Little did I know then that circumstances would take such a turn that a move to a new yard was to become absolutely essential.

Premonition

It is claimed that emotional problems can result in physical conditions. If this is true, is it any wonder that Jazz would develop a problem with her heart?

My sense that Jazz was going to fall ill as we travelled abroad was so strong that I had even mentioned it to a few people, including my daughter. As I stood in the field with Jazz the day before our holiday, my tears fell into her soft coat. She turned to nuzzle me, and I felt ashamed. I shouldn't be burdening her with my worries and concerns, but I knew my intuition was telling me something, and I had never been like this before. We had holidayed many times over the years, never for longer than a week, but although sad to say goodbye, I never had any concerns, knowing that she would be safe and well when I returned. But this time was different.

"Well, are you picking up on anything physically wrong?" someone had asked me, when I had told them about my fears. And that was the thing. Physically, even though she was eighteen, she had more energy than ever before. With

her tendency to bounce and jog, she was actually becoming very difficult to hack out. Just days before, she had given a very good depiction of a horse from The Spanish Riding School, with her "airs above the ground", cantering on the spot, and showing off her ability to hold a really good levade (a low rear). None of this was asked for, mind you. It was the result of someone dismounting from their horse in front of us, causing her to back up the bridlepath at the rate of knots. A quick dismount on my part resulted in her imitations of a Spanish riding horse, as I held the reins either side of her.

So no, there was absolutely nothing going on with her that would set off any warning lights. But there was no dismissing the fears in my heart. As we flew to Madeira, I had to give myself a very good talking to. There is a saying which I love: *"Change what you can, accept what you can't, and be smart enough to know the difference."* And this was definitely one of those times when I couldn't change what was about to happen.

My spiritual wisdom was coming to my aid. I knew I had to let my fears go and not ruin the holiday. After all, there was nothing I could do. It was out of my hands! I had to enjoy the holiday and make the most of spending time with my husband and children. After all, now that they were 22 and 20, there may soon come a time when they choose not to come away with us; so I needed to really embrace this time with my family and be grateful for it. All I could do was pray to God and the angels that my horse would be fine, trusting that it would be so.

Four days later when my phone rang, I was prepared. There was no shock! It transpired that the UK was still suffering the same blasting heatwave that had started a few days before our holiday. The horses had been coming in the stables during the day to escape the heat, but Sam who ran the yard and was looking after Jazz for me, was concerned about her. Although she had seemed fine on the morning, she hadn't wanted her tea, and she seemed stiff and uncomfortable. "Should she get the vet?" she wondered. *"Yes, definitely."* I replied *"There was clearly something wrong."*

To cut a long story short, Jazz was a lot worse by the time the vet arrived, and she had to be rushed to hospital. She was sweating profusely, and her readings were very worrying. It transpired that she had a great deal of inflammation around her heart and lungs, and pneumonia was suspected although never proven. She spent ten days in hospital, and her illness was put down to a viral infection. The atrial fibrillation, which now blights her life, means that she has been retired as a riding horse; but better that than putting her through risky procedures. I could never risk Jazz's life just so I could ride her.

Energy healing

Experiences in the past have demonstrated that out of great suffering can come miracles, so I was determined to keep the faith! I knew this was happening for a reason, and I knew that I needed to stay vigilant. All would become clear. I was convinced of it.

Before the miracle could reveal itself, further calamity struck! Both my daughter and I contracted covid. I had been separated from my horse for the ten days she was in hospital. She had only been home for three days, and now I was forced to separate from her again for another ten days.

I was beside myself! All this care and attention she needed, and I was being forced to hand her care over to someone else.

Day one in isolation, I made a promise. I could drown in self-pity, fear, or worry, or I could use the time more productively. I chose the latter!

During the next ten days, I re-connected to my spiritual centre, spending time listening to spiritual podcasts, meditations and books. I made up for not being physically present with my horse by sending her reiki healing. My fear was replaced by hope, as well as a deep knowing. My horse would be fine!

As a healer, I absolutely believe in the idea that the more people who send healing, the more it is amplified. So many people were sending love, healing and prayers to Jazz. One special group in particular connected to the energy in her photograph, and for three weeks running, on a specific day and time, directed healing to her.

What I witnessed over the next few weeks just astonished me.

Physically, Jazz was doing amazingly well. She was eating better than normal, and as well as looking in good shape, there were some surprising physical changes. The lump on her back leg, arising the previous year from a fractured splint bone, had disappeared, as had the lump on the front of her face, which had been there for the nine years she had been with me. The farrier on his visit, declared her to be the "best ever" on her legs, in the nine years he had shod her.

Mentally and emotionally, she was doing great as well. The brightness in her eyes reflected her happy demeanour, and everyone was commenting on it.

Whenever she has experienced illness/injuries in the past, the excessive "stable rest" has always proven problematic. But not this time! A more willing patient it would have been hard to find. She accepted the first few days of very limited paddock turnout with good grace and willingness. Even with just thirty minutes turnout, she was neighing and coming when called. Not once did she turn away when taking her medicine. Wow, even human patients aren't this good! The whole time, she just radiated peace and calm.

Then there was the love. It was emanating from her like a brilliant beam of light.

The yard manager, who cared for her in my absence, recounted tales of her whinnying and trotting over to her as soon as she spotted her car. She was won over by her demonstrations of love and beautiful behavior. Even I could barely believe it when, out in her paddock, she greeted the farrier with a huge neigh as he rolled up in his van and walked over to him. I know he is kindness itself, but this is still the man who has to hold her in uncomfortable positions.

Then there was the love she showered on the hospital staff, on her return checkup visit (three weeks after being released from hospital). As I led her off the horsebox, amidst the roar of bulldozers (they were extending the carpark), I could barely recognise my sensitive, flighty thoroughbred. She walked away with one of the vet assistants, relaxed, chilled, head lowered, and ears pricked, and amazingly she didn't even glance at the machines making all this noise.

A couple of hours later, the head vet would recount how Jazz remembered each and every one of them, greeting them as they entered her stable. The vet explained how it had taken some time to lead her back to me, as she insisted on saying hello/goodbye to every single horse. I felt grateful to the vet for allowing this, as I know how they must be constantly working against the clock. The vet exclaimed how Jazz had won them all over with her endearing attitude and her interest in everything. So much so, he promised me a discount on the next visit. She had made their day!

They had also made mine. The scans were good, showing that structurally her heart was back to normal. She did still have atrial fibrillation, but in my heart, I knew this already. I felt that my horse was fulfilling her destiny. She might be retiring from ridden work, but there are other roles to step into, not least that she gives me huge inspiration with my writing.

The next day, instead of being returned to the medical paddock where she had been since her illness, she was led down to her own field. It was like returning a queen to her subjects. Her neighbours each took turns to come to the fence, greeting her warmly and affectionately. The next day, as I led her to the field, the horses all lined up along the fence line, whinnying their greeting when we were some distance away. What a welcome party!

Just a week later, someone on the yard confided in me how much their horse was calmed by Jazz's presence, and they certainly know about it when Jazz isn't there – be it either in the stable or field.

Sometimes it takes a tragedy to realise what you have got. Sometimes it takes a calamity and a complete unravelling of what is normal and routine, to take you into the realms of something magical. Sometimes it takes love and healing from others to create a miracle.

Is it possible I wonder, for a person/animal to absorb all the love and healing sent to them, and reflect it back outwards? As I considered the events of summer 2021, it certainly seemed that way.

New yard for Jazz

It quickly became apparent that Jazz was not going to tolerate being returned to her normal field, despite having a close friendship with the horses either side of her. She had always been uneasy about being so close to the tree line, although previously this had only been a problem in the winter. But not anymore!

On a few occasions, she would go crazy when being led out of her field, rearing up until the rope pulled through my hands. Then she would proceed to gallop up and down the track, at speeds so fast that she just resembled a blur. At nine years old, I had always been bemused by the fact that her dad had been a fantastic racehorse who had won over £200,000 in prize money, as Jazz always seemed quite slow compared to most horses, but at eighteen she was something else. It seemed ironic in a way. I had always worked on her suppleness and agility to keep her strong and fit for as long as possible, but even though she seemed more agile than ever, her heart condition had now put paid to any riding work.

So Jazz was returned back to the medical paddock, while I waited for a space to come up at Rosie's yard. Thankfully, we didn't have to wait long, and Jazz was soon happily ensconced in the field with the horse she has a great deal of respect and admiration for. In short, it was a match made in heaven! Surprisingly, Rosie, with her kind, gentle heart, appeared to be the leader, and this was a first for Jazz. I am always struck by Rosie's gentle manner with Jazz, and Jazz's incredible ability, as always, to read the situation. Her social skills are incredible, and as with Rosie, it is probably down to the fact that they grew up on a stud farm. So theirs is a harmonious, peaceful friendship and with the enigmatic thoroughbred, Fred, in the adjoining field, they have made a beautiful threesome. Although very close, neither of them as much as raises their head when you take one out the field without the other. It is lovely to see this level of trust and independence.

As is very clear from this chapter, like us, your animal doesn't have to be a saint to be spiritually evolved. We all have the shadow side as well as the light, and animals too, are trying to overcome these negative aspects to their personality. We are all on the journey to enlightenment, and this is true for our animals as well as for ourselves. I like to think that I have helped further Jazz's spiritual progression as much as she has helped mine. And isn't this true of the animal/human partnership when experienced at the deepest level. We are all here to help each other!

A self-reflection exercise

- Give yourself time to reflect, making sure there are no distractions and you won't be disturbed.

- Start to connect to your breath, taking deep breaths in through the nose, and out through the mouth.

- When you are fully relaxed, think about one of your animals and consider what their soul purpose may be for coming to Planet Earth. Most domestic animals are here to help us on our soul journey, by offering us unconditional love, joy and support. So firstly, think about what qualities your animal has brought into your life. If they are challenging, think about why this might be so. Maybe they are trying to teach you to have more patience, or to be a better listener, or to give them quality time. Maybe they are mirroring something in yourself which needs addressing.

- Once you have identified the gifts or challenges they have brought into your life, consider how you can best support them in their soul mission. What changes can you make to help your animal achieve their purpose? If they are here to advance your spiritual progression, then think about learning Animal Communication or becoming Reiki attuned. You could really push the boat out, and sit with them pen and journal in hand to see if they want to channel a book through you. If they want you to connect more to joy, then think what activities you could employ to facilitate this.

- If there are challenges, consider how you could do things differently. For instance, if they leave you feeling frustrated, consider what changes you need to make which would allow for a positive outcome. Maybe you just need to spend some quiet time with them, just connecting through meditation and through the heart, allowing them to feel your gratitude for them being in your life. If you open your heart to your animal, they in turn will open up towards you.

Try to remember that it is no accident that your animal has picked you to be their Guardian. Feel grateful for this, and try and honour your animal's soul purpose by collaborating with them as much as you possibly can.

HARRY

A Lesson in Respect and Spiritual Growth

*"Throughout history
Man has used animals for his own ends.
Yet the animal who has acquiesced so humbly
Is the same one
To propel Man on his evolutionary journey"*

Harry' story is very powerful, because it not only raises questions around respect, but it also throws a spotlight on how we expect animals to just accept things that we would never, ever accept for ourselves.

This really does highlight how our treatment of animals is so very different to how we would treat other humans. *"Yes"* people will say *"But they are animals, so it is different?"* Maybe, although when you really stop and think about it, is it really that different? We have been brainwashed into thinking it is so, but when you step out of that conditioned way of thinking and look at it objectively, you realise that we have one set of rules for us and another for animals. At the end of the day, respect should be a two way thing, and should apply to everyone equally, whether they are animal or human. This is something we have not yet fully grasped.

I have lost count of the number of times that people refer to a horse as being disrespectful because he has stepped into their space, or has taken a hold when led to the field, but how respectful are we in our treatment of them?

Harry, bless him, was going to give us a lesson in the art of respect. But he also had another remarkable teaching. Like my horse Tiffany, he would go on to demonstrate how animals can be a catalyst for our own spiritual growth and evolution.

In all of this, there was also going to be a very powerful lesson for me too, as I would have to face up to the realisation that my ego was running the show.

Harry the puppy

I first met Harry when he was a young puppy. My friend Kerry had acquired this beautiful Rhodesian Ridgeback from the same breeder as her older dog, George. Not only was he from the same breeder, but he was also from the same pedigree line. Having had huge showing success with her older dog, she was hoping that Harry would prove to be just as successful. From a physical perspective, this puppy was as perfect as it is possible to be, so his potential as a successful show dog was enormous.

Even in those early days, Kerry was doing everything to prepare Harry for the show ring. It was all going well until the time came for him to be handled and inspected by strangers, when he started to make it very clear that he was not happy with this invasion of his boundaries. I agreed to carry out an Animal Communication with him to find out what was going on, and why he was objecting. His success as a show dog hung in the balance.

Meeting Harry for the first time, I was really struck by the beautiful, big star emblazoned across his chest.

When I carried out the Animal Communication with him, it was impressed upon me that his star marking was hugely significant. From a Biblical point of view, the star represents a sign from God to follow His path. In this respect, it is a physical representation of Harry's connection to the higher vibrational energies and celestial beings. Could this path be for my friend Kerry? Yes, Harry confirmed. He had very much entered Kerry's life to lead her down the spiritual path.

In that first connection with him, I was really struck by his sensitive and spiritual nature. It also made a lot of sense to me that he had come into Kerry's life to help her walk down the spiritual path. Kerry is hugely clairvoyant, but until now my attempts to encourage her to undergo some formal spiritual training had fallen on deaf ears. So in my mind my interpretation of the communication was thus: this dog was going to lead my friend away from the showing world, freeing up her time to develop her spiritual skills, and allowing her to step onto her true path.

My chat with Harry had really opened my eyes to what we sometimes mindlessly put our animals through. When I asked him why he didn't like strangers touching him, his indignant response was, *"These people are very rude. How dare they touch me without asking permission first. How would you like a stranger to just walk up and put their hands on you? And not just a friendly pat either. They are putting their hands where I would much rather they didn't. It is rude and disrespectful. People need to have a deeper respect and regard for dogs, as too many just see us as commodities, rather than sensitive, feeling and sentient Beings."* Well what could I say! He certainly had a point.

Harry the show dog

Kerry persevered as best she could with helping Harry reach his potential. She was attending many ringcraft classes with him, and a handful of shows. But things always fell apart when it came to the judge handling and inspecting the dogs. Harry would fidget and struggle to stand still, and it was very clear that he was struggling to cope with it.

My friend is a Capricorn, and like me, she doesn't give in very easily. She tried all manner of things: aromatherapy, dog behaviourists and dog whisperers. But things were going downhill pretty quickly. The final straw came just a few weeks short of his first birthday.

My friend had taken him to an event run by a Dog Whisperer, which was aimed at dogs with showing issues. What transpired resulted in my friend being on the brink of packing it all in. Her dog had become really upset, barking at the dog whisperer and shaking all over. All attempts to calm him were futile. She was told that her dog was reacting worse than any dog this dog whisperer had ever come across, and she left the event seriously questioning whether it was right to put him through this a moment longer. She rang me to talk it over.

I have to confess that I had been so blindsided by my original communication with Harry that in my mind I was convinced that my friend would need to give up showing completely if she was to walk down the spiritual path. I am ashamed to admit it, but this thinking had stopped me offering to carry out a Reiki session on him. After all, how could it possibly work? My friend was to be led away from showing and so winning classes would not allow this to unfold. Also, I always ask for Reiki to work at the highest good for the animal and Guardian. Winning showing classes is very much an ego pastime, and has no soul benefit whatsoever. If I carried out Reiki and it failed, then my friend would be disillusioned and even less inclined to further her spiritual journey.

But the conversation with my friend that day changed my thinking. None of us like to see our loved ones sad and disillusioned with life. As she talked about how she had tried just about everything to get her dog to stand for the judge, I had to be honest with her - and also with myself. It was my ego that was preventing me from offering to carry out a Reiki session with him. What right had I to determine who should or shouldn't have Reiki? And what right had I to assume the outcome? I suddenly found myself saying, *"There is one thing you haven't tried: Reiki. Let me carry out a distance Reiki session on him."*

The power of Reiki

We arranged a distance Reiki session for the Wednesday evening. I also gave my friend some exercises to carry out (see end of chapter). Finally, I stressed the importance of carrying the right energy when they were in the ring together. I explained to my friend that as the judge walked towards them, she needed to be very mindful of the pictures in her head (see it all going swimmingly well) and to try and be as calm and relaxed as possible, breathing deeply.

The reiki session went well and it felt very powerful. The next day, my friend remarked that Harry had been so sleepy that he had literally fallen asleep on his feet. She had been amazed by this, and claimed to have never seen this happen to a dog before. This sleepiness all happened about 24 hours after the Reiki healing. It is claimed that Reiki can have effect for three days afterwards, so it was not necessarily surprising.

Excited about seeing whether or not it would work, my friend arranged to go to a big County show on the Saturday! From the moment we arranged it, I just seemed to know it would work; as did my friend! And maybe this helped as much as the Reiki, for we both had total belief in it. That belief was completely justified. Harry won his puppy class as well as Best in Breed. For the first time ever, he was relaxed and calm, standing perfectly happily for the judge. We were both over the moon!

Two weeks later, my friend had a Crufts winner on her hands. A few days before, I had carried out the same distance healing on him. Her dad who accompanied her to this huge show just couldn't believe he was the same dog. Calm, focussed and self-assured, he was a worthy winner, again standing just beautifully for the judge.

To say my friend was bowled over is an understatement. She couldn't believe how her dog had gone from "Zero to hero" in just a few short weeks. It all felt completely surreal for her and she was in a state of complete wonderment. *"You have proven how miraculous this Reiki is, I have to get attuned myself. I am going to book on the next available course"* she declared. I smiled at this statement as the truth hit home. This dog was leading my friend well and truly down the spiritual path; just in a different way to how I anticipated. What a lesson for me!

But in true Reiki fashion, it wasn't winning the competitions that had brought my friend the greatest happiness. She had always enjoyed a close, loving relationship with her dog, but she admitted that the soul to soul conversing and the meditations she had shared with him were helping her to bond with him on a much deeper level. Most of her training up until this moment had focused on desensitisation, but now she felt she had taken a huge step beyond this. In working on the deeper soul levels, she was finding that their connection was becoming more telepathic and she was starting to give him instructions through the mind rather than the voice.

Just to prove this was all no coincidence, the next show my friend took her dog to, there was no Reiki carried out. The result? Not good. Her dog growled at the judge (in a frightened way, not aggressively) and had to be taken out of the ring. A couple of weeks later, he attended another show. This time I carried out some distance healing on him, and he won. There was a very clear pattern here which did not escape my friend's notice. *"The quicker I am Reiki attuned the better"* stated my friend. *"I can't keep asking you to do it."*

The following year, my friend became Reiki attuned. She described the attunement as one of the most beautiful experiences of her life. She reckoned the peace and love that surrounded and infused her was beyond anything she had ever experienced before. It was deeply affecting for her, in much the same way as my attunement had been for me. From that moment on, she routinely gave Harry healing before his showing classes.

I feel that sharing Reiki with your animal really deepens the bond, and that it helps them trust you and understand that you have their best interests in mind. This certainly seemed to be the case with Harry, who has grown from strength to strength. He now understands that the handling is all part of the package. His trust in Kerry, and his confidence in the ring has really enabled him to step into the great showing dog he always had the potential to be. As I write this, he has just become a champion, having won three major championships.

But more importantly than his show dog role, he has been able to fulfil his spiritual purpose, for Kerry is now well and truly walking the spiritual path. All thanks to Harry!

Exercises to carry out

I set out below some exercises I gave Kerry to carry out. These are useful if you are competing with an animal, as they allow for relaxation. Not only will they help the animal to relax, but they will also help you to relax. This is so important, because the animal feeds off your energy. If you are scared, it will frighten them also, and will put them into fight, flight or freeze mode.

- In the days leading up to the show, spend time with your animal. Talk to them and explain what will happen. Animals understand way more than we give them credit for, because even if they don't understand the words, they do grasp the energy behind the words, and this can give them big clues as to what might happen. It can really prepare them.

- Perhaps also take the time to carry out some peaceful meditations with your animal. This will not only create some beautiful energy between you, but it will also help to strengthen your bond and connection. They will start to trust you more. In these gentle sessions, you could put a few drops of lavender on a tissue. Dogs in particular, see the world through their nose, so if they can associate the lavender with relaxation, it may help to put some on a tissue before going into the ring.

- When you are at the show, be very mindful of how your animal is dealing with it. How can you make it enjoyable for them? Before you go in the ring, spend time connecting with them and focusing your energy completely on them. Talk to them, give them scratches/massages, help them to relax and connect deeply with them. Form pictures in your head of what is going to happen and try sharing these with them telepathically. Visualise what will happen and imagine it all going really well. As you do so, also feel the emotions of happiness and joy.

- When you are in the ring with your animal, be extremely mindful of your energy, the thoughts in your head and what you are projecting. It is important to breathe deeply and envisage the very best outcome you can. Visualisation is so important. This is recognised by top competitors who regularly use visualisation as part of their preparation process.

A self-reflection exercise

- Give yourself some time alone. Take a few deep breaths and get into a very peaceful state.

- Think about your animal and try and put yourself into their paws/hooves etc. Imagine you are them, and think about how you feel treated. Do you feel there is a lack of respect in some area of your life? For example, if it is a horse, do you feel that permission should be given before a rider climbs on to your back? After all, you may feel unwell. How could you get this across?

You could set a whole day aside, where you try to see things from your animal's perspective, by imagining you are them.

These exercises will actually wake you up to seeing just how little choice our animals have in their lives. They are completely dependent on us to make the right decisions for them.

This is a powerful exercise and it will certainly give you food for thought!

SILVER

A Lesson in Joy

*"Joy is always there for the taking.
It is not something that lives outside yourself,
No, rather it is an integral part of you
Which can get buried under the layers of life.
But remember, it can be resurrected at any time.
Always it is a matter of choice
And only you can decide."*

The moment we cast our eyes on Silver, a beautiful 14.2hh Connemara gelding, we knew he was the one.

It had been on our minds for some time that Lauren, my daughter, needed to move on to a bigger pony. But we couldn't bear to sell her outgrown pony Chelsea, so we decided that she would go on loan to someone we knew, while we had a bigger pony on loan.

Silver was the first pony we looked at, and as he raised his head to look at us as we drove into the yard, an overpowering feeling of connection washed over me.

I have always been able to read energies of people and animals very easily, and as we were introduced to Silver, I was well aware of his happy-go-lucky nature. Here was a pony who felt joy effortlessly.

The next five years were spent blissfully with this amazing pony. Just seeing his beautiful head in greeting over the stable door every morning would send my spirits soaring and put a smile on my face. We were truly blessed that his wonderful owner entrusted him to our care.

It is hard to express how incredible those five years were spent with Silver. He was such a generous, kind and characterful pony. His most favourite thing was galloping across country, jumping fences, so he loved fun rides and Hunter trials.

Although he found flatwork a bit boring, he did enjoy dressage competitions and showing off his talent. And he certainly knew how to wow the judges. Many a time, as he came down the centre line overflowing with charisma and presence, I would gasp at the transformation in him. How could an ordinary pony look so incredible! I clearly wasn't the only one to think it either, as on a few occasions the judge came out to speak to us. We were encouraged to affiliate him, and Lauren was invited to join BYRDS (British Young Riders Dressage Scheme), but we didn't really have the time. We both felt that it was important to keep things light and fun, and not take it too seriously. And Silver was most definitely having fun. For whenever he caught sight of a lowered horsebox ramp, he would be trying to drag you up it. His adventurous spirit just loved outings; until he had to have an x-ray on his mouth, and then he wasn't so keen. But a few fun ride outings soon got him running on to the box again.

Silver showed huge talent for dressage. Winning both his Pony Club area classes, he took Lauren all the way to the Pony Club championships, where they performed a lovely test. He won his first elementary dressage competition with 70%, but sadly, even though his work was improving, it would prove to be his last test. For he had a bone growth in his mouth, and this along with the growing melanomas around his throat, meant that his head carriage had become unstable - fine for normal riding, but not dressage.

With Lauren off to university, we advertised for a rider who would be able to exercise him while Lauren was away. The Universe was about to step in and create a wonderful opportunity for someone. In fact, Silver was about to change someone's life.

A life-saving opportunity

A young woman who responded to our advert, seemed absolutely perfect. She clicked with Silver immediately, and the deal was done. She would be his new rider.

I often rode out with her on Jazz, and once she had known me for a few months, she confessed something quite incredible. It turned out that she had been suffering terrible depression for over a year, and had barely left the house in that time. But she just happened to see our advert, and talked herself into responding to it. Like us, she adored Silver, and she actually credited him with saving her life. For now she had managed to wean herself off the anti-depressants, and she had got her life back on track. Silver's joy was just infectious and it had re-energised her. She now realised that she had much to live for! Even now, a few years on, she claims that Silver saved her life.

I love how the Universe enabled this to happen and the synchronicities that were involved. The final ingredient was Silver's magic. He knew how to breathe the life back into a weary soul.

Infected Melanoma

About six months after Lauren started university, we were contacted by Silver's Guardian. It was time for him to return home.

Thankfully, his Guardian didn't live too far away from us and so we still kept in close contact with him, and in the holidays my daughter visited and rode him regularly.

Just a week or so into the summer holidays of 2019, we learned that Silver had a problem. He had suffered with melanomas for years – around his throat and underneath his tail - but now they had discovered a large internal one in his sheath. He was in pain and his sheath was badly swollen. In addition, it was causing some nasty infections. He had been put on strong painkillers and antibiotics, but with surgery not an option due to its size and position, his future looked uncertain. In the words of the vet, he was a ticking time-bomb. Not only that, the melanomas around his throat had also grown considerably.

It was devastating news. Even though he was 18, his work was still improving. In terms of ability and fitness, we felt he hadn't yet peaked.

On a beautiful summer's morning, I accompanied my daughter on a visit to see him, the intention being to carry out some Reiki healing. The vet was coming to assess him the next day, and my daughter was worried he might be put to sleep. It could be our last visit!

With great sadness we arrived at the yard. Silver had been put in the stable, and he greeted us with his usual nicker. After a fuss and scratch, I started giving him Reiki. Just five minutes working on his heart chakra, he was yawning, licking and chewing. I moved one hand on to his wither, and the other on to his shoulder. As the energy flowed, I started to become aware of his energy state. It wasn't what I expected! Rather than feeling depressed and down, he felt incredibly happy and joyful, and this was flowing through to me. My head started to fill with messages. *"Live in joy. Life is too short to do otherwise. Don't cripple yourself with negativity. Run with the wind and feel it. Happiness is a choice and it is always waiting there for you, even when you are facing the worst. Don't waste the time you have left in sadness. Your state of mind is always a choice, and I am choosing happiness."*

His joy was permeating every part of my being. I heard his request to be surrounded by joyful memories – an easy request to fulfil. Over the years he had provided us with many wonderful memories and so there were lots to choose from. As these flowed through my mind, I felt overcome with gratitude. This amazing pony had brought all my daughter's dreams to life, and just the sight of his beautiful, alert face every day would fill us with happiness and joy.

After the Reiki, we spent time with him. He made us laugh as he charged around everywhere, diving on the best bits of grass while Lauren water-skied behind him. And he made his polite requests for treats, which we happily obliged. We spent time taking photos, while he posed beautifully; his big character and personality captured so perfectly. It was impossible to take a bad picture of Silver.

Finally, the time came to say our goodbyes. As we walked away, I turned to look at his beautiful, attentive face, watching our every move. This was the moment my heart was supposed to break into a thousand pieces. This was the time I was supposed to drown in tears. For it might be the last time I looked into those gorgeous, big, kind and loving eyes. So why was I feeling such joy? Why such happiness? Why did I feel like a young girl wanting to run around the fields in ecstasy? What on Earth was happening here?

As I struggled to make sense of it, I heard those immortal words in my head, *"Don't cry for what you have lost, smile for what you have gained and for the beautiful memories we have made. They can never be taken away. We have so much to be thankful for."*

This wonderful pony had taught me the meaning of joy that day and he had demonstrated that even when there appears to be dark clouds ahead, you can still choose to feel joy. It felt ironic really. I had turned up to visit him that day hoping to give him some healing, yet the tables were turned and I was the one who had been healed. This just demonstrates how Reiki is a two way thing. It is something shared, and in that sharing, both parties can receive something positive.

But Silver's story was about to take a very different turn.

Joy lost

A couple of weeks after we had visited him, Silver's Guardian was extremely worried about him.

The vet had assessed him the day after our visit, and it wasn't good news. She reckoned the big golf size lump in his sheath, was 99% likely to be a melanoma, and there was very little that could be done to help him. The size and position meant it could not be operated on, and it seemed inevitable that he would continue to suffer with recurring infections. She also mentioned that if he was hers, she would probably have him put to sleep, for this seemed the kindest option.

Two weeks on from this, Silver certainly seemed to be a pony who had lost his joy for life. His Guardian, Vicky, was extremely worried about him. No longer the happy-go-lucky pony, when in his stable, he would just stand and stare at the back wall. There was no doubt in everyone's mind that he was thoroughly miserable.

Vicky could not get the words of the vet out of her mind. Would it be the kindest thing to put him to sleep? He was most certainly not himself, and quite understandably the vet and Vicky were interpreting his depressed mood as the result of pain. As he had always been a very stoic pony, the concern was that he was feeling a high level of pain.

It was agreed that I would go over and see him, have a chat, and try and establish what it was that Silver himself wanted. Was he ready to go, or did he have a bit more fight in him? I would also give him some Reiki healing.

The healing session

Arriving at the yard, it was indeed distressing to witness the change in Silver's demeanour. Like Vicky had reported, he was indeed standing in the stable with his head facing the wall. Even our arrival at his stable hardly warranted any interest. He seemed oblivious to our presence. This was not a Silver I had ever encountered before, and it was just heart-breaking to witness. I totally understood why Vicky considered him to be suffering.

But, as I started to meditate and let my energy converge with his, I was totally shocked by what he revealed. It seemed that it wasn't pain that was making him depressed, but the possibility that his life hung in the balance. He made it very clear that he was aware that he may be put to sleep, and he was just not ready for this yet. It wasn't his time! He went on to explain that he would make it very clear when he had had enough. His refusal to eat his bucket food and treats that were offered to him would be sign enough that life was unbearable. And he wasn't there yet!

As I recounted all this to Vicky standing outside his stable, the tears streamed down her face. I sensed her relief that he was not yet prepared to give up the fight.

Following this revelation, I proceeded to let the Reiki flow through me. Putting my hands gently on Silver, I let the Reiki flow for as long as it was needed. It may have been 20 or 30 minutes later, but Silver started to yawn excessively. He must have yawned about ten times. I felt a huge release, and it seemed the appropriate time to end the session. There seemed to be a change in Silver's energy. Was it my imagination, or did he seem more interested in us and his surroundings? There felt a definite change. I hoped I was right.

Miracle healing

The next day we received the most amazing news.

Vicky could not believe the change in him. He had spent most of the day cantering around his field. Our joyful Silver was back!

A few days later, his spirits were still so high, that Vicky asked if Lauren would go over and take him a little ride. She was really keen to see how he would react under saddle.

The change in him could not be put down to imagination. He was without doubt a pony who was now full of beans – more like a four year old than an 18 year old. He jogged the whole ride, and Lauren had to work her hardest to keep him calm and under control.

The lifting of his spirits had worked magic on all of us. He had given such a clear answer to our question, and Vicky was now prepared to do everything to prolong his life.

I also wanted to pull out all the stops. Being a big believer in the idea that the more people who send prayers/healing, the more powerful the effect, I posted his picture on various healing Facebook sites, and asked people if they could all please send him prayers and healing. There must have been about 100 people who responded, and I was so grateful for each and every one of them.

My belief in the power of positive thinking was well founded. As the months proceeded, Vicky was noticing that the lump in his sheath was shrinking. By Christmas, we couldn't feel it at all. This was just incredible! He had not been treated with anything else, and with the vet 99% certain that it was a melanoma, it just seemed simply miraculous. How was this possible?

Nearly three years on, it does seem highly likely that Silver has internal melanomas. They are very large around his throat, which does restrict his airways somewhat, and so with this, and obvious signs that he is uncomfortable with a rider on his back in canter, he has been retired from riding.

He is on borrowed time, but the important thing is that he is still a pony full of joy and still enjoying his life to the full. He has not had a depressive state since I sent him the Reiki in the summer of 2019.

When Lauren gets chance, we pop over to see him. He always raises his head at our car turning into the yard, and he always walks over to Lauren in greeting. They love playing together in the menage, and Silver always gets very excitable indeed. He follows her like glue as they walk, and run around the menage together, acting like a playful pup as he gallops and bucks, kicking up his heels in sheer delight at their exuberant game.

"Remember" he says. *"Life is for living. When you are prepared to seek out joy, you will find it."*

Postscript

Very sadly, a month after writing Silver's chapter, we received some devastating news. Silver had impaction colic and a displacement. Things weren't looking good for him.

Lauren headed over to see him straight after work, and was able to spend a few hours with him. I sent him some distance Reiki, with the intention that whichever way things would go, it would help him.

I also picked a card from my Animal Tarot deck and asked for information regarding Silver. Was it his time to transition? I felt it was, but I needed to see what the Universe would tell me. The moment I saw the card, there was no doubting the answer.

The card was The World card, and it depicted a sheepdog sitting on a plinth with wheels (in the form of the eternity symbol). Around the dog was a wreath (association with death) and seven butterflies (a symbol of transformation). The circular wreath along with the word "World" gave me the impression of life having come full circle and being complete.

The words on the card seemed so appropriate. "Congratulations on successfully accomplishing what you set out to do! You've made it through the challenges and incorporated the lessons life offered you with grace and courage." There is no denying that Silver had displayed immense grace and courage throughout his life. Just to connect it even more to Silver, the card also depicted two objects (possibly recorders) at the dog's feet. The one was gold and the other silver.

I had my answer, but at least it had been delivered to me in a very positive and uplifting way. For it was lovely to know that Silver's soul had achieved everything it had come here to do, and he had lived a truly successful life. The message, together with the beautiful picture on the front of the card, brought me a great deal of comfort.

The following morning when I rang his Guardian, she tearfully explained that although Silver was acting normal with his head over the door and ears pricked, when the vet examined him she discovered that his small intestine was twisted. She was absolutely gobsmacked as normally this would cause a horse incredible pain, resulting in them rolling or thrashing about. She declared that never in her years of being a vet had she ever come across a pony so brave, acting like nothing was wrong. I like to think that the Reiki I had given him had helped, but knowing Silver's stoicism and courage, this probably had a lot to do with it as well.

There was no alternative but to put Silver to sleep. This beautiful boy, who had touched so many with his lion's heart and soul, was getting ready to kick his heels up over Rainbow Bridge. He may have moved on to pastures new, but I like to think that his essence of joy will live on, not only in the hearts of those lucky to have known him, but in those reading his story immortalised in this book.

RIP gorgeous boy and thank you for showing us how to live!

Your exercise in joy

- Give yourself time to reflect, making sure there are no distractions and you won't be disturbed.

- Start to connect to your breath, taking deep breaths in through the nose, and out through the mouth.

- When you are fully relaxed, ask yourself the question, *"Where in my life could I create more joy?"* Take the first thing that comes up for you.

- Think about what steps you could take, to have more joy in whatever situation has come up for you. Put some changes in place and set out an action plan, whereby you could incorporate a small step towards creating joy each day. Remember it all starts with thought, so build up towards joy by thinking positive and recalling happy memories.

- We all find joy through different things, but the following are some ways you could create joy. Try to commit yourself to engaging in at least one joyful practice every day:-

    Listen to some upbeat music and dance wildly to it. Release the joy from within.

Do something fun and exciting with your animal. Something you will both really enjoy.

Take a walk in nature and really connect to your senses, of sight, hearing, smell and feel. Appreciate the beauty and look for things you may never have noticed before, such as the rainbow colours reflected from the sun in the dew soaked fields. When I first set out on my spiritual quest, I was amazed at how many rainbows are created out in nature, and I just couldn't believe I had been so blind before.

If you are creative, what can you do that will make you happy? I have discovered my joy in writing, and enjoy writing blogs and books.

If you have young children, engage in a really crazy activity with them and release your Inner Child.

Do something charitable or in service to others. This can bring great happiness and fulfilment.

Read an uplifting and joyful book.

Watch an uplifting film or comedy.

Spend quality time with loved ones.

Engage in spiritual practices which further your connection to the divine. Animal Communication and Reiki healing really help me to connect to a high vibration of divine love, bringing me incredible peace and joy. I really can't get enough of these practices.

THE LAST GOODBYE
(A tribute to Silver who transitioned in 2022)

As you lay your head to sleep
I pray you cannot hear me weep.
To hear you neigh just one more time
A gift like that would be sublime.

Lent to us, you were a gift
Our spirits you would gently lift.
Upon your back you let us ride
We thrilled to the beat of your powerful stride.

What I would give for one more day
Listening peacefully as you eat your hay.
The brush of whiskers across my face
Thundering hooves as you pick up pace.

Oh, precious horse you cannot see
How very much you meant to me.
Your heart was big, your foot so sure,
The love you gave, forever pure.

I see your body lying cold
No experience of growing old.
Your time on Earth was meant to be
A wondrous song, a melody.

Like flowers that dance merrily upon the Earth
The memories you leave are fill of mirth.
To keep us going through the darkest night,
Precious jewels to ease our plight.

I thank you for the gifts you brought
The many lessons that you taught
Humbled by your gentle soul,
You touched my spirit, and made me whole.

Your legacy, it will live on,
For no life is lost or ever gone.
Your heart forever entwined with mine
Hoof beats of love across all time.

PART 2 – ANIMALS GIVEN SECOND CHANCES

*"Treasure your life
And the lives of those around you,
As a gift bestowed on the worthy.
Every life is as valuable as the next.
There is no distinction."*

Animals are often at our mercy. Not just the wild or farmed animals, but domestic animals too can have a precarious hold on life, as man is prone to taking on a godlike role in deciding whether an animal should live or die. This is a huge responsibility for us as Humans, and one that we don't fully appreciate. Often times, we give little thought to the power our decisions wield.

When an animal is old or ill, it is much easier to make the decision to euthanize, sparing them from a debilitating illness, or a slow agonising death. In these circumstances, there can be no argument really against the decision to put a suffering animal out of its misery. Most of us wish we too could be spared the indignity and pain of a drawn out passing.

Other times, a decision to end an animal's life can be much harder to justify. It is at these times that we need to look really deep into the reasons behind our decisions. We need to stand back and question whether we are seeing things as they really are, or are we seeing through the lens of our own perception. Lots of questions need to be asked. Is it really in the best interests of the animal to euthanise? Should the animal be given the chance of a new home with a new person?

With horses for instance, I have seen so many act and behave completely differently with a new person. Many stories abound of the horse who was considered highly dangerous and unpredictable, yet with someone else they changed into a pussy-cat. People who witness such transformations are forever in wonder of how this is possible. Sometimes all these animals needed was a new start, with a fresh outlook, surrounded by a different energy.

In this section of the book, you will read the stories of three animals (a dog, horse and cat) who fit this criteria. They came very close to being euthanized, not because they were old or ill, but because they were considered mentally unfit to cope with life. In all three cases, it was considered kinder to end their mental torture, than for them to suffer the torment of their daily lives.

In Watson's story, we are forced to recognise the degree of empathy our animals can experience. When animals like him take on our own thoughts, feelings and emotions to the degree he did, then not only will this negatively impact their life, but it can also endanger it. His story is very powerful and there are many lessons for us to take away from it.

Many horses are considered mad, bad and dangerous, but Max's story demonstrates perfectly that many of these horses are just frightened and scared, having been badly let down by the humans in their life. When you dig deep, you often find a horse with a beautiful, sensitive soul, whose gentle nature is just waiting to be uncovered. Max's story is the story of too many horses. We need to do better by them!

It is claimed that kittens have to be socialised when they are very young to stand any chance of accepting human contact, but there are exceptions to this rule. Tinkerbell's story falls into this category, revealing that the desire to communicate at the deeper levels is innate in all of us. Her story also has an added teaching; letting go of our desire to control outcomes allows our animals to fulfil their soul destiny. Sometimes, we just have to honour their wishes!

The stories of animals such as these are incredibly important. We are asked to dig deep and really consider what is best for our animals. Do we know them as much as we think we do? Is the situation really as hopeless as we perceive? When we have exhausted all the normal channels, maybe the solution lies down a new and unexplored track. Maybe we just need to step back and look at the bigger picture. Do we really have the right to dictate their future and play God with their lives?

The animals I have chosen to write about all responded really well to reiki healing, and they all went on to lead very happy and fulfilling lives. Additionally, they all brought deep and profound love to the people whose lives they entered. It was like they recognised that they had been snatched from the jaws of death, and in return they embodied intense grace and gratitude, touching those who loved them with a really special energy. They went from the traumatised to the transformer. To all those witnessing these changes, it is nothing short of miraculous.

It takes great courage and humility to accept that an animal may be better off with someone else. But accepting this can be the greatest gift of love you can give to an animal and the consequences can be truly transformational. Not just for the animal, but for the person whose life they go on to grace. Everyone is a winner!

WATSON

A Lesson in Transformation

*"For every problem there is a solution.
As long as you have faith, courage and belief
The answer will reveal itself"*

In the years I have been carrying out Animal Communication and Reiki healing, I have seen some incredible transformations in the animals I have worked with, but the changes I witnessed in Watson in the space of a few short weeks were nothing short of miraculous.

Watson's story is incredibly inspiring, and it also carries some very powerful messages. There is so much we can all take away from reading his story, and hopefully it will also help other animals who may be in a similar situation. I always say that whatever problem an animal may have, there is always a solution. It is just finding it. At times this may mean venturing off the beaten track, but believe me when I say the answer is there. You just haven't found it yet. Watson's story demonstrates this beautifully.

I first met Watson on 29/12/2021. Our meeting had been arranged, and I was lucky enough to spend three hours with this utterly gorgeous Rhodesian Ridgeback dog.

Arriving at my friend's house with his new Guardian, he walked in confidently. He was a stunning dog, and there was absolutely nothing in his demeanour or his behaviour to suggest that he was anything but a happy, self-assured, confident and well-balanced dog. Here he was in a strange house, with strange people, yet he happily introduced himself to my friend and myself. In the three hours I spent with him, I never saw the slightest anxiety or unease.

Yet, only four weeks previously, Watson was a very different dog to the dog who stood before me now. So different in fact, that it seems almost impossible that he could be one and the same dog. I have never before witnessed such a change in anyone, be it human or animal.

Watson was a dog who had always been loved, adored and well-cared for. He was not a rescue, and as far as anyone knew, he had not suffered from any trauma or any known medical condition. Yet from the age of 15 months, he had started showing the first signs of fear, anxiety and panic attacks. These escalated so much, that by the age of four he had seen numerous vets, behaviourists, and he had been prescribed various drugs, of which he had been on the highest dosage it was possible to prescribe.

His Guardians were doing everything possible to help him and it was breaking their hearts in the process. Whenever they made changes to try and help, there would be some improvement initially, but then he would decline. By the age of 4½, they were desperate and beside themselves. They just felt they had run out of options.

By this point, Watson was in a really bad way. Despite the high dosage of drugs, he was having about ten panic attacks a day. His Guardians were unable to leave him, even though he had another dog for company, and he was keeping them up every night with his anxiety. They hadn't slept properly in months. They felt he was continuously agitated and ill at ease. He was lethargic, and showed no interest in anything, neither wanting to play with them or their other dog. He rarely wagged his tail and didn't even acknowledge his name. They recognised that here was a dog who had no joy for life, and for whom life was just difficult. It was heartbreaking to witness, and they were beginning to feel that they may have no choice other than to put him to sleep. Understandably, they couldn't bear to see him suffer this way, and ending his life was beginning to feel like the only option left.

But thankfully, they did something which would save his life. They sent an email to the woman who had helped the breeder in his early life and they poured out his story to her. Philomena immediately agreed to pick him up and offered him a home with her. Having six dogs herself, she did say it might only be a temporary solution until she could find a suitable permanent home. But clearly this would all depend on whether Watson could be helped and relieved of his suffering. At best, she envisaged that it would possibly take a year before he was mentally strong enough to cope with a move to a forever home.

I first heard Watson's story about a week after Philomena had picked him up. My friend Kerry had called me asking if I would please carry out some distance Reiki healing on Watson and also an Animal Communication to find out what had triggered his anxiety in the first place. My friend's words were *"I have seen this dog and he is such a sad soul. His anxiety is off the scale. He will be a really challenging case, but I can sense he is such a loving dog. If you can crack this, it will be a true miracle."*

My friend Kerry is also Reiki attuned, so it was agreed that she would carry out Reiki on him in person at the same time as I sent him some distance Reiki healing. I agreed with Kerry. We had to try everything we could to help this dog. No animal deserves to suffer!

Reiki healing

It was an evening in early December 2021, when I sat down to carry out the Reiki healing.

The photograph that Philomena had sent me of Watson had been taken about a week earlier. I used this to connect with Watson's energy and to send him the distance healing.

The session felt good, and I just let the Reiki flow from my hands.

There were some questions that Philomena wished to ask him, but looking deep into Watson's eyes on the photo, I found myself struggling to connect with his soul essence. His eyes seemed empty and expressionless, and the feeling was like I had come across a blank wall that I just couldn't break through. Intuitively I knew why. The high dosage of drugs had disconnected his soul from his body. It was like he just wasn't there.

I realised that I wouldn't be able to carry out an Animal Communication using my normal method of connecting and conversing with the soul of the animal. So instead, I asked the Universe, angels and spirit Guides if they could please give me the information I required, by showing me things which would answer Philomena's questions.

The first thing that became evident was how loving a dog Watson was and is. The majority of dogs bless us with their ability to give us unconditional love, but somehow the dial seemed to have been turned up with Watson. He was so loving and empathic that it had been his downfall.

A lot of people don't realise that empathy is a quality that is as evident within our animals as it is within us; we tend to think of it as unique to humans. But this is just not true! Many animals can display this beautiful quality too, and as with people, it can prove to be very problematic and confusing for them. I actually think that with the sensitivity that animals possess, many of them are highly empathetic, and I have lost count of the number of people who tell me how their horse, dog or cat knows instinctively when they are upset, needing a loving cuddle. Many animals are highly tuned to our moods, emotions and even our thoughts. More so than we could ever know!

In my head, playing out like a movie, I saw a picture of Watson as a young puppy, playing rough and tumble with his male guardian. Next, I felt his pain when this member of his family started spending long periods of time away from home. For Watson, this felt like abandonment, and he couldn't understand why a close member of his family would choose to stay away. In a dog's world, loved ones stick together! It turns out that this man was in the army, so yes, he was required to spend long periods of time away.

Now this could be unsettling for many dogs, but for a dog as loving and empathic as Watson, it was even harder to deal with. Relative to ours, dog lives are short, so six months away from home can seem like a lifetime to a dog.

This felt like the trigger for Watson's anxiety, followed by time spent in army barracks, and lots of comings and goings. As his anxiety started to increase, then so did the concern of his Guardians. They started to worry and stress about him, and Watson, being so empathic, was taking on their emotions as his own. Not only did he have his own emotions to contend with, but he had theirs to deal with also.

So the escalation of fear and anxiety started to build like a snowball, until Watson was having full blown panic attacks. The fear, worry and guilt his Guardians were experiencing was just fuelling Watson's own anxiety and distress because this is what happens when you are an empath. You take on other peoples'/animals' emotions as if they are your own.

So, I had been given an explanation for his anxiety. The next question had to be, could he be helped? What could Philomena do to help him heal?

In response to the first question, I immediately received some very positive signs. I saw a picture of Watson having been slowly weaned off all the drugs, and having done so, I saw his energy and joy of life returning. His soul seemed returned to his body.

I asked the Universe whether Watson would be healed, and I asked for the answer to be revealed in a card from my beautiful Animal Tarot deck. The moment I turned the card over, I breathed a sigh of relief. I had received a very positive message indeed!

The card was entitled, "The Lovers" and it featured two flamingos, their necks craned together forming the shape of a heart, with a butterfly flying over their head. This was an auspicious sign! The butterfly points towards transformation, and the flamingos symbolise finding true love. The message in the booklet also mentioned the healing of past wounds and a return to good health. All of this felt very uplifting, and together with the beautiful feeling of peace and serenity from the card, it very much seemed to be pointing towards a good outcome. I felt optimistic!

My optimism soared over the next 24 hours. My Facebook pages suddenly seemed to be full of stories concerning traumatised, anxious and panic-stricken dogs who had overcome their problems to become well-balanced and happy. I passed this on to Philomena. The signs were good!

As for the question of what Philomena could do to help him, I was downloaded with various bits of information.

Watson had received this Reiki healing from myself and Kerry, but he was also receiving some in-person Reiki healing from another friend of Philomena's. It was fantastic that there were three of us giving him this healing, as the power of Reiki is a bit like the power of prayer: the more people who give it, the more it is strengthened, and the more effective it has the potential to be. I sensed that this had really helped him.

I also gave Philomena a meditative exercise to do with him. Just spending some peaceful time with your animal, where you connect to beautiful, divine energy, can be very peaceful and restorative. Not just for your animal, but for you as well.

It was also important that Philomena didn't feel sad or anxious for him, because he would just pick up on these energies and take them on as his own. Feeling these things would just drag him down. I advised her to see him as whole, healed and healthy, and to reassure him that he was safe, loved, and had nothing to fear. Looking deep into his eyes when she said these words, would help him understand what she was trying to convey.

Finally, I picked a card. What advice could the Universe give Philomena?

The card was Giraffe Spirit, and it was very much encouraging her to see things from a higher vantage point. When we are prepared to really open our mind, and to look for answers in those harder and higher to reach places, then solutions can be found. Sometimes we just have to venture off the well-worn, beaten track to find them. I felt this was particularly poignant for Philomena, as Animal Communication and Reiki healing were practices she had never before encountered. She was already following the advice in the card, by being prepared to open her mind and experience things that were totally new to her.

The truth is that Philomena had already fallen madly in love with this dog, and she was prepared to try just anything to help him. This is typical for a lot of people. They have tried just about everything, but the love for their animal stretches their mind in ways they couldn't possibly have envisaged. And through that stretching, they discover the magical solution. This can be the catalyst for a completely changed perception.

The meeting

I offered to give Watson further Reiki if it was required but, amazingly, it proved not to be necessary.

By the time I met Watson nearly four weeks later, he was doing incredibly well; better than anyone could have anticipated.

He had been completely weaned off the drugs. Not only had the panic attacks ceased altogether, but the anxiety and edginess that had been his constant companions were nowhere to be seen.

When I was shown a video of Watson leaping, playing and having fun with some doggy friends, I could have cried with joy. His spirit and his love of life had returned, and it was so wonderful to witness.

But now Philomena had a really big question to consider. Watson had been offered a wonderful home with his breeder. He had been to her home a couple of times with Philomena and had really enjoyed his time there playing with the other dogs. Philomena felt this lady could offer him the very best life and could give him things she couldn't. For a start, it was a beautiful big house in the country, with lots of land for the dogs to play and run around in. Added to which, they would never be left for any time at all, because someone was always at home. He would have everything that a dog could wish for.

But obviously the question to ask was, *"Could Watson cope with another new home so soon after becoming so well settled into his life with her?"* His transformation had been so complete and miraculous that Philomena was terrified of doing anything that might set him back. Would it be a step too far? She had been expecting not to have to make this decision for about a year, so being faced with it now, after only four weeks together, felt like too much too soon. Would it be the straw to break the camel's back?

It was an interesting dilemma. When the question was first put to me, my first initial reaction was one of horror. We were dealing with a dog who had serious abandonment/trust issues, so another move so soon after the first one just seemed a recipe for disaster. There was the potential here to undo all the good that had been done.

Thankfully, I have learned to overcome the fearful ego thinking, and embrace a wholly different perspective. My belief in Reiki and creating positive energy has proven to me time and time again that when we embrace these ways of being, events can really take a very different turn. Surrounding people/animals/events with peaceful, loving energy can really transform them.

So with this in mind, I was prepared to see things differently, and to open my mind to a different outcome.

It was agreed that we should meditate with Watson, and the question in everyone's mind should be put to him. How did he feel about this move?

Philomena was also very anxious for him to know how much she loved him, and for him to know that she would be there for him every step of the way. Very sensibly, she had put in some steps for him to make the adjustment gradually. He had already been to visit the breeder a couple of times with her. She had arranged to leave him there for four hours to see how he would cope. If that went well, then an overnight stay was in order. But she also wanted to reassure him that if he wasn't happy at any stage of the proceedings, then he could just stay with her.

Meditating with Watson

Watson was lying down on a blanket. Philomena sat behind him, Kerry in front of him, me on his right side, and Philomena's 11 year old daughter and their other dog sat on the settee behind Kerry. We were all set!

The quiet time with Watson was simply blissful. His eyes were closed throughout, and the energy surrounding him can only be described as beautifully peaceful and loving. As our energies merged, I was struck by the love and gratitude this dog exuded. He absolutely understood and appreciated everything that we were all doing for him, and his energy was touching each and every one of us. So much so that we were all in tears!

Watson made it clear to me that he trusted Philomena's judgement completely. She had brought him this far in a few short weeks, and now he was ready to trust and go along with any plans that she had for his future. All was well in his world.

The next bit of information almost blew me apart. In the first Reiki healing session a few weeks previously, I had picked up that Watson had a very strong crown chakra. In other words, he was clearly a very evolved, spiritual dog. But I hadn't realised just how advanced he was on his soul path. For now, I was struck by the idea that this whole episode had been part of Watson's soul plan for coming to Earth. At the soul level, everything was happening and playing out exactly as Watson had intended it. Not only had he opened peoples' eyes to the efficacy of Reiki healing, but his story was going to be a big part of my book. Through reading his story, many more people would have their eyes opened as to what is possible outside conventional treatments. By reaching out in this way, he would be touching many peoples' hearts and minds.

Finally, I wiped away my tears and said my goodbyes to Watson.

Driving home, I felt such elation and happiness that I had met Watson and had been able to spend a few hours with him. It felt like an incredible blessing! So much so, that he dominated my thoughts for a long time afterwards.

The forever home

A week later, I contacted Kerry to see how things were going for him.

It turned out that his overnight stay (a few days after our meeting) was so successful, that he just stayed. Things couldn't have worked out better. Another week on, there has been no signs of anxiety, and wonder of wonders, Watson has fallen in love with one of the bitches.

Wowzers! Can it get any better! The flamingo card (The Lovers) was absolutely spot on – not only with his healing, but also with him finding his love for life, as well as meeting the love of his life.

The whole story is like a fairytale. Watson has found his forever home! I just love happy endings and this story really couldn't get any better.

Messages to takeaway

There are so many powerful elements to Watson's story. If he really did come into this physical dimension to pass on some important teachings, then we need to take on board some of the lessons he is trying to get across.

Firstly, and probably the main thing, is that we should never give up on our animals. There is always a solution, even if it is not immediately obvious. We just need to stretch our thinking and our perceptions. In fact, this is a lesson that my own horse Jazz had for me. In following paths off the beaten tracks, we are expanding the mind and venturing into areas that are beyond left brain logical thinking. We live in a world of infinite possibility, but instead our society has wrongly brainwashed us into thinking that we live in a world of separation, scarcity and random events. Is it any wonder that so many people struggle with life when they are faced with such depressing concepts?

It also highlights our dependence on medicines and drugs, which as Watson's story demonstrates, can be doing a lot of damage to us. In Watson's case, he had become completely disconnected from his very self and his identity, and his joy for life had completely dissipated.

It is so easy to just hand out drugs, but these just act like a sticking plaster, and don't actually deal with the wounds underneath. It is so important that the root cause is addressed. This applies to people just as much as it applies to animals. I would love to see a more wholesome healthcare system, where holistic and conventional medicine is integrated, and where preventive healthcare is also available. The mind and body are so closely related, and yet we don't fully appreciate how much this is true.

Finally, I just love how all the characters in his story, were all so courageous and selfless. Each and every one of them only had his best interests at heart, and they all worked together to try and find a solution. So much can be achieved when people join together like this. The power of this love, which was able to overcome the darkness of fear, made a great ending inevitable.

It goes without saying that I feel incredibly blessed to be part (even if it was only a small part) of Watson's story. There were a couple of nights, when I was so excited by the unravelling of events that I could barely sleep. This is how I wish every animal's story would end.

"Watson, you have touched so many hearts with your courage and grace. You deserve now to live out the rest of your Earthly life in peace, joy and love. May all of God's blessings be on you and all those who have loved and cared for you."

A self-reflection exercise

- Give yourself some time alone. Take a few deep breaths and get into a very peaceful state.

- Start to reflect on an animal(s) in your life. Is there anywhere that you are holding on to some fear in relation to any aspect of their life? Are you fearful regarding a health issue, or a behaviour?

- If you identify any fear, think about how you could reframe it. Work on yourself, so that you learn to let go of the fear and take steps which will enable you to think more positively.

The thing is, fear serves no purpose whatsoever, and it doesn't help our animals. At worse, it will be a block to healing and/or finding a solution; and our animals being the sentient, sensitive and often empathic souls they are, will often take on our fear as their own, with disastrous consequences.

That said, it is easier said than done to let go of fear. I too, have been there many times with my own animals. But knowing how much it hinders their progress, I now try really hard to let it go.

You need to find what works for you. I try to have faith and belief in the idea that things are happening for a reason, and everything is playing out the way it is supposed to. My animal may have chosen to go through this for their soul growth, or even for my own soul growth. When we realise that we are eternal beings who have come to planet Earth for a short time to learn lessons and to evolve, then life becomes much easier. You also start to see the hidden treasures in events that we would normally perceive as negative.

Just remember, nothing is ever as it seems.

MAX

A Lesson in the Power of Love

*"For some there is no second chance,
But I was the lucky one!
In time, I would reward the courage which saved me
By offering my heart and soul.
There is no greater act of love
Than stepping in to save a stranger."*

All of us at some time or another have been grossly misunderstood. Let's face it, nobody really knows what is going on behind the image we choose to present to the world. Many people's outward appearance does not match the person they really are on the inside. It is the same for horses too. The only difference being that when we are misunderstood, we don't lose our life over it.

In many ways, Max's story is quite shocking. Like many horses that have gone before him, and many, no doubt that will follow him, his is a story of gross misunderstanding. This horse had been written off as mad, bad and dangerous, when in truth he was just a sensitive, scared and frightened horse. Sadly, this is the story for way too many horses.

But Max had luck on his side, something that many horses are denied. I think luck is the wrong word to use – more like perfect synchronicity, because I truly believe that he was meant to be in the life of the young woman who stepped in to save him. I very much believe in the idea that we have soul contracts with others before coming to Earth; be it with people and/or animals, and Kate stepping in to save Max without a second thought is great evidence of the soul bond that existed between them.

In time, the selflessness of Kate's actions would allow this horse to reveal his true colours. Once his cloak of fear was stripped away, he was able to reveal his true, luminous Being – a very gentle, sensitive, empathic and intuitive soul with an incredibly loving heart. It seemed he had many gifts for Kate, and in saving him, she was in part saving herself.

Little did Kate know what a journey she was to embark on when she stepped in that day in July 2014 to save a horse she barely knew. She was at the yard where she kept her horse, when a vet turned up announcing that he had come to put a horse to sleep, and he asked for the horse to be pointed out to him. It transpired that the horse was on loan to a couple of people, who had conveyed to the owner that the horse was dangerous and needed to be euthanised. This was on the grounds that he had knocked over the older lady when she went in to the field with a bucket, breaking her arm in the process.

But what do you expect, if you enter a field of four horses with a bucket? It is kind of obvious that it isn't going to end well. Max was to pay a heavy price for something he may not even have been responsible for, because there was some confusion as to whether he was the one who had knocked her over. For whatever reason though, he was the one singled out!

Kate describes how she had no idea what came over her. She just stepped in and offered to buy the horse without a moment's consideration. So when the loaner finally turned up at the yard, it was agreed that if the owner was willing, Kate would take on this horse as her own.

Deal done, Kate became the new owner. The owner was understandably wary, because she had been given a strong impression from the loaners that he was unpredictable, so she agreed to let Kate have him for a two month provisional period to see how things worked out. The owner of the yard was understandably concerned as well, and he warned Kate that any bad behaviour from this horse would result in them being thrown off the yard.

It seemed that everyone just believed everything they had been told about this horse, without getting to know him and to make their own minds up about him - the exception being Kate and myself, who could just see straight through to his big, beautiful heart.

Animal Communication

I was deeply in awe of how Kate had stepped in to save him, and felt immensely grateful that she had been there when the vet arrived, giving her the opportunity to give this beautiful horse a new life.

I had just been attuned to Reiki 2 healing, and I needed a case study. It had already been agreed with my teacher that I could use horses for my case studies, as she knew how passionately devoted I was to them, and she knew that my future work was with animals. So now I asked Kate if Max could be one of my case studies.

Thankfully, Kate agreed, so I immediately carried out an Animal Communication on him, to find out more about his personality, character and what he could tell us about his life so far.

Like Kate, I knew very little about this horse, other than what had been said about him. I too kept my horse on this yard, but it was a fairly large yard, and I had never really seen the loaners do much with him, as they had seemed more interested in the three horses they owned. However, I had witnessed the blacksmith trying to shoe him and through that witness I saw a great deal of pressure being applied to a scared horse. Something that would never end well! Sure enough, they decided to give up and put him back in the field. It was clearly the case of a fearful horse, made more so by the treatment that was being handed out to him.

When I tuned into Max, I was immediately struck by his gentle, sensitive nature, and I could sense that he had a very loving heart. There was no doubting that he was a noble horse, possessing immense generosity of spirit, with no grudges or bitterness about what had happened. I am always humbled by the love these animals show, and their lack of judgement.

Many of the things he told me, Kate was later able to validate. He had been bred to race, but never did. He had passed through the hands of many people, and some of these had been very inexperienced, causing him to lose confidence and lose trust in people's abilities to make good choices for him. Kate later found out that one well-meaning person had placed him in a field with a stallion, causing him to be badly beaten up.

It was no surprise to discover that he was a very bad cribbiter – the endorphins released in his brain when he carried out this activity helped relieve his crippling anxiety and stress.

It was clear that Max understood everything that had transpired and he was fully aware that Kate had saved him from the jaws of death. Although exceedingly grateful to her, the whole unfortunate event had caused a great deal of shock and trauma.

I asked him to pick a card from my *"Way of the Horse"* oracle card deck" (Linda Kohanov). What did he want Kate to know about how best to handle him? When I turned the card over it was "Eye of the Storm." Max was giving us a lot of information through this card. The card depicts waves, rearing like horses as the storm surges forward, but the eye in the centre looks calmly towards the shore. I instantly knew what he was trying to convey with this card. In response to his fearful reactions, he just needed Kate to be calm and unruffled, acknowledging his highly strung emotions as merely information in the moment. There was no need to panic in response to his strong feelings. She just needed to be the anchor to his storm. Easier said than done of course, but in time Kate would recognise how very sensitive he was to her thoughts and emotions, and she would learn to dig deep and find the inner calm within herself. Like any journey within, it would take time for her to find this inner calm and serenity.

What was very clear from the communication I had carried out with Max is that he was a horse in desperate need of some Reiki healing. There were many layers of pain that he needed to shed, and much fear and anxiety which needed to be overcome. But I knew without a shadow of doubt that in time he would be a loving companion to Kate. As well as this, I instinctively felt that he had come into her life to help with her soul growth, and that ultimately she would be empowered through her connection with him.

Reiki healing

It was agreed that we would offer him some Reiki healing straight away.

The last time that Max had been brought into the barn was when the blacksmith had been attempting to shoe him, so now Max had bad associations with the barn, as it was just triggering those memories of being dominated, and reminding him of his fear. This was not a place where he felt safe.

So it was no surprise that for our first healing session, Max had to be treated in his field, because he really did not want to come into the barn. Could the Reiki help him let go of his fears and traumas of the past? I sincerely hoped so, because in a few short months he would need to come into the barn to be stabled at night.

I expected the Reiki to go well with Max and I was not disappointed. The sensitive thoroughbreds respond really well to it, and Max was no exception. He seemed to lap it up, standing quietly and happily while I worked all over his body. I also let Max choose where he wanted it to go, and he offered his back, and his head to me, making it clear that these were the places that he wanted my hands placed on him. The knowledge also came to me that we should use another horse as a surrogate mum to him, acting as a lead into the barn.

The first Reiki session had resulted in some positive changes to Max, and allowing him to follow the other horse into the barn worked like a dream. Just a week later, you wouldn't have recognised Max as the same horse. He was standing quietly, and was fine to groom and have his feet picked out. In no time at all, he no longer needed the other horse and was happy to come into the barn on his own.

But a big test was coming up: he needed his feet attending to. Following on from the fiasco the last time the blacksmith visited him, I knew that he was in need of another Reiki session to prepare him.

This time I carried out the Reiki session in the barn. Like the first time, Max really enjoyed the session, soaking up the peaceful energy, and enjoying the soulful connection. He offered his back, shoulders and head for me to work on, and by the end he was letting out some really big sighs. We took the extra precaution of helping him relax, by allowing him to watch some other horses being shod and giving him a lick.

Kate and I couldn't have been more pleased with him. There wasn't too much needing doing with his feet, but he had remained calm and accepting throughout. It helped that we have a really kind, considerate blacksmith who is just so calm and understanding with the horses he works with. This was such a great start! The second session with the blacksmith went equally well.

Three steps forwards, two steps back

I would love to say that Max was a reformed horse and his fear just melted away in a few Reiki sessions, but that was not to be his story.

His fear and trauma ran so very deeply that his healing would take time. Also his very close soul bond with Kate, and his highly empathic nature, meant that he would be greatly affected by Kate's moods and emotions.

Kate discovered that those days she arrived at the yard in the morning, stressed and in a hurry to get to work, were the exact same days where he would keep stopping and refusing to move forwards. She laughs about it now, recalling those days where they would end up going backwards all the way to the field. Forwards a problem, but backwards was just effortless. Maybe he just wanted to keep his eyes on Kate!

Winter at that yard meant the horses came in at night into their stables. Max didn't particularly like coming out of his field in the dark. He could also be problematic going through the two gates that had to be navigated; bombing through them like he was experiencing an electric shock. Maybe he had received a shock from the electric fencing in the past, or maybe he had been hit with the handle on the tape. To get around this, it was easier to attach a long lead line to him, so that when he tried to bolt, there was plenty of room to manoeuvre him. As soon as he was through the second gate, he would walk into his stable quietly.

A new home

Eventually, Kate arrived at the decision of making a new start on a new yard. She sensed that Max seemed upset when the loaners were around. Those were always the times when he would become anxious and uncooperative. It certainly seemed to be the case, although there is no ruling out the possibility that these were also the times that Kate felt more on edge and uncomfortable, and Max being the empathic horse he is, was picking up on her energy and reacting to it.

The decision was made. A new yard beckoned!

Sadly, things didn't turn out well on the next yard. It was a track system, and Max was accused of bullying another horse. Kate never witnessed this, and it was just hearsay, but they were designated a field away from the other horses. Once again, Max was perceived negatively by the other horse-owners. This time he was accused of being a rig (showing stallion like behaviour), and the same solution was put forwards - he should be put to sleep because he was clearly a danger to others.

There was no alternative but to move again. On the next yard, Max was much happier, but Kate's other horse was not. So another move was made.

Finally, they arrived at a place where everyone was happy. The fields and stables are set in some beautiful, secluded countryside, surrounded by trees. Whenever I visit, I am always struck by the calm, peaceful energy. It is a little oasis! It has proven to be the perfect place for Max to heal.

Kate took on a small Blue Cross rescue pony, and she accredits him with reigniting Max's love of life. Max grew really attached to this small, cheeky pony, and their ensuing, close friendship allowed him to rediscover his playfulness, and to learn to be a horse again.

Soulful horse

Whenever I visit Kate, I am always struck by Max's independence and his desire to connect with us.

The first time I visited, which was about a year after their move, Max came over and chose to stand with us, despite the rest of the herd wandering off to another field. As he stood sleeping, with my hands lightly resting on his shoulder, he seemed to be really soaking up our high vibrational spiritual talk. About an hour later, he woke up, stretching and yawning. All three of us soaked up the beautiful energy that appeared to be flowing in to us that day. It truly was a beautiful connection!

In the ensuing years, Max has always seemed to enjoy these times of connection. In my most recent visit, I spent about an hour stroking and fussing him. From time to time, he would turn his hindquarters on me so that I could scratch his rump. Ever the gentle horse, he would quietly present those areas of himself where he required attention.

Kate was quick to point out that Max is not like this with anyone else who visits. On the contrary, he seems to dislike new people coming into his space and will actively avoid them. As I pointed out to Kate, I am the exception because he knows how much I love him. And I do! In my eyes he will always be a very special horse, as he put his trust in me in those early days, opening his heart to the reiki and AC I was offering him. He took a leap of faith in those days despite his trauma, and I will always respect his strength, courage and willingness to allow us to help him.

Kate recounted those times when he would instinctively know she was down and upset about something. Like a mother comforting her beloved child, he would always be the first one on the scene to offer his love and solace, placing his head in her lap. Once Kate had soaked up his sympathy, he would invite her to play, reminding her that life doesn't have to be stressful. *"Life is for kicking your heels up and having fun"* he would remind her.

On one very memorable occasion, when Max was offering his love and support, he actually offered something really sacred. Pushing her with his nose, he directed her to his back, leaving Kate in no doubt whatsoever that he was actually inviting her on to his back. Accepting his graceful invitation to *"Let's go ride"*, Kate found somewhere to mount, swinging her leg over him. Walking around the field with just the headcollar to guide him, they proceeded to amble around the field for the next half hour; two gentle souls in perfect harmony, connected through the heart.

This was such a special moment for Kate, because her intention had never been to ride him and she had never done so until this moment. Putting her own needs and wants aside, she hadn't felt that it was in Max's interest to be ridden. He had suffered enough trauma over the years, and she also felt that he didn't have the best conformation to withstand having a rider on his back. Such is the qualities of a true horsewoman – to put the horse before herself! In the ensuing years however, there have been times when she has popped on his back for an amble around the field, and Max is never anything but the true gentleman, taking really good care of this special woman.

The other remarkable thing about Max is the friendship he offered to Kate's young sister. When very young, like most young children, this small child could sometimes find life a bit overwhelming, reflected in outbursts of temper tantrums. But Max loved this little girl, and those times when she needed a friend, he would always be there for her; holding her and supporting her through her inner turmoil. His love was returned in bucket loads, resulting in this young girl bringing up her teddies to show him. When she was old enough to do so, she would sit and read her books to him. Max would delight in this connection, and was never anything other than utterly gentle. As with Kate, he would happily trundle around the field with her on his back.

Needless to say, it was not the small ponies that the little girl favoured. No, much rather the 15.2hh thoroughbred! He was the one who had won her heart. Kate admitted that the bond they shared deeply awed her. Because in those early days with Max, she openly admits that he sometimes scared her with his fear fuelled antics, but around her sister he was never anything but utterly calm and gentle.

Reflection

On visiting Kate and her herd of horses a few days ago, we reflected on how far Max has come.

We talked about those early days when he was so anxious and fearful. Although the Reiki healing had helped him initially, there were still many layers of trauma that this beautiful horse had to shed.

The fear has long gone out of this horse's eyes. Now all you ever see is a gentle softness; the true essence of his soulful Being.

Kate reckons that he is probably the easiest of all her horses. Golden to load on a horsebox, quiet for the blacksmith, dentist and vet, there are no indications of the anxiety these people used to cause him. He is even great to take his wormer syringe. Kate just explains to him that he needs to take it for his health, and it will be over quickly, and he just happily obliges by acquiescing sweetly to what is being asked.

I agree with Kate's observation that Max's soul seems to grow ever brighter. He is a true luminous soul!

As we reminisce over Max's life, Kate becomes enamoured with how far they have come together, and the huge changes in Max. She had forgotten just how traumatised and fearful he had been in those early days. As the memories return, Kate lights up, recognising that it is their loving connection that has brought them where they are today. So much can be achieved with true, unconditional love. It is the greatest alchemy of all!

I ask Kate what she thinks have been Max's greatest lessons for her.

Without a moment's hesitation, Kate replies that he has taught her a lot about self-love and self-worth.

The moment these words are uttered, I can't help but draw a sharp breath. For I had been reading my case study notes the night before, in anticipation of writing this chapter, and on the first day communication I had carried out with Max, when I asked him what message he had for Kate, I had heard a song playing in my head, *"The Greatest Love of All"* by Whitney Houston. Anyone familiar with this song will know that the words describe how the greatest love of all is with yourself. In choosing this song for Kate, Max was actually giving us a really big clue as to why he had come into her life – to remind her just how wonderful and selfless a Human Being she is and how important it is to recognise her worth. He wanted her to love herself like he did, recognising that he is offering a mirror to her radiant soul. How she sees him is how he sees her!

This journey with Max has really taught Kate to value herself and to trust her own instincts. Only she knew what was right for this horse, allowing the fear to recede from his eyes, to be replaced with the gentle softness that is a true reflection of his character. It has been a wild journey at times, but they have overcome the bumps in the road, to find true transformation and alchemy. It is these journeys which hold the greatest healing, not only for the animal, but for the human Guardian too. She gifted him with life, and he in turn has repaid her courage, enabling her to feel self-love and self- worth. Like all soul relationships, they have saved each other!

A self-reflection exercise

- Give yourself some time alone. Take a few deep breaths and get into a very peaceful state.

- Start to reflect on an animal(s) in your life who is acting badly. Think about how they are acting out and try and put yourself in their paws/hooves. Could they be acting badly out of fear? Or pain? Or could they be mirroring your own energy?

- Try and think about how you could react differently to the situation i.e.. Rather than reacting negatively, try being the calm eye in the storm. Could you just sit quietly with them, offering them calm, peaceful, loving energy? Would they benefit from Reiki healing? How could you help them conquer their fear, and what supportive steps could you put in place? What changes do you need to make to your own energy? What changes do you need to make to your thoughts about them?

Just remember that when animals act badly, they are often doing so because they are worried, fearful, frustrated, in pain, or because they are reacting to our own energy. It is down to us to offer them a refuge; a place where they feel safe, be that a physical environment, or the strength of our own heart and soul.

A self-love exercise

This is something we all struggle with. Constantly comparing ourself to others, we often feel that we don't match up. It is a massive problem, and the world would be so much better if we all learned to love ourselves.

I would love every child who walked through the school gates to be told every day that they are special, and they have unique gifts and talents to bring into the world. Just imagine how different our world would be if every child felt valued and loved.

The truth is this; to have true balance in the world, we all need to respect our differences. For example, a good talker needs a good listener. But it doesn't mean that one quality is any better than another. They are all of equal value. Know that your part in the script of life matters, and you have a part to play. You are just one aspect of the divinity that shines through us all.

Have a go at this self-love exercise, and see where you are falling short and need to give yourself a bit more love. Your animal will love you shining some light of awareness on yourself, as they will benefit from it too.

- Give yourself some time alone. Take a few deep breaths and get into a very peaceful state.

- Ask yourself where in your life you feel that you come up short and are not good enough?

- Take on the role of counsellor. What would you say to yourself regarding the list of things you have come up with.

- It is always important to look at things from a different perspective. So as a counsellor, how could you put a different spin on it? Don't be afraid to really think outside the box.

- Now that you see it differently, what actions can you take to turn these perceived negative aspects of yourself, into something positive, allowing yourself to feel good about them?

TINKERBELL (TINKY)

A lesson in honouring another's journey

*We have this innate compulsion to control
Along with an overwhelming desire to force outcomes.
In trying to make life fit into our projection of how we think it should be
We can be causing much misery to another.
Instead, it is much better to go with the flow, allowing the soul
To play out the story it intended for its physical incarnation.*
"

It is said that there is a small window of opportunity to socialise kittens. If they are not socialised within a certain time frame, then they will never accept human contact. The experience my daughter and I had with a feral cat has made me question this belief, and I do now believe that there are exceptions to this rule. Tinkerbell was one of them.

It was around 2013, when people on the yard we kept our horses on started reporting seeing flashes of a white cat. To start with, the sightings were so brief, that people were questioning whether they had really seen a flash of white out of the corner of their eye, or whether it was just their imagination. But as more and more people started reporting seeing a flash of white cat, it did seem certain that this was something tangible, and not imagination. Could there be a feral cat hanging around the yard?

At the time of the sighting, another cat, Teddy, had taken up residence at the yard; but Teddy was a different kettle of fish entirely. There was no doubting with him that he was very much a domestic cat. He was extremely friendly, and in beautiful health and condition. Attempts were made to locate his owners, but despite carrying out the appropriate enquiries, he was never claimed.

Teddy was living in one of the feed rooms at the yard, and we were all making sure that his needs were being met. A cat bed was acquired, and cat food was being left at regular intervals for him. But over a couple of months it started to become obvious that Teddy was sharing his food and bedding with a friend. The white cat had started to materialise, and touchingly, it seemed that Teddy had taken her under his wing. In actual fact, this new cat was not wholly white. She had a lot of white in her coat, but also some brown and black too.

My daughter named the cat Tinkerbell (we called her Tinky for short), which seemed appropriate given her prettiness and gentle energy. Lauren also made it her mission to try and tame this cat, recognising the need to take it very slowly and appreciating it would take a long time. She was happy to take as long as it took.

Over the coming months, when food was put in the outbuilding for the cats, we would just observe, and to start with it was enough for Tinkerbell to just be aware of our presence. No attempt was made to go near her because we didn't want to frighten her.

But Teddy just loved fuss and attention, so as soon as he had his fill, he would come around rubbing against our legs and we would stroke him, as he squirmed in delight under our hands. As we did this, I was always intrigued by Tinkerbell's reaction. It was obvious that she craved the stroking and fuss too. She would start rubbing herself against the bins, like she was imagining herself being stroked. I could sense that she absolutely craved this attention, but her fear was a huge block to getting what she wished for; but it did make me believe that this cat could be tamed. There was hope!

Lauren was extremely patient. As Tinkerbell ate, she would edge ever closer, until Tinkerbell was actually letting her touch her. Lauren was extremely gentle, just stroking her with one finger to start with, and any sign of anxiety on Tinkerbell's part, she would withdraw her finger, but we were encouraged by her growing confidence.

We had fallen big time for our new cat. She was so gentle and sweet. It was becoming clear that she desired the same connection that we had with Teddy. I could so clearly see the love this cat had to give, and in time we would come to recognise that this was no fantastical whim.

Rescue cat

Tinkerbell had been at the yard a few months when we discovered how she had arrived there.

One of the women on the yard worked for an animal sanctuary, and it turned out that they had taken Tinkerbell in when they found her living rough with a litter of kittens. She was absolutely traumatised by her enforced capture; so much so, that she refused to eat or drink anything if people were around her. Such was her distress that sadly they decided to take her kittens away from her because they didn't want them affected by her trauma. I can't even imagine the terror she must have endured by having had her beautiful kittens taken away, not knowing what had become of them.

It was felt that her fear was so great that the only alternative would be to put her to sleep, but the lady on our yard came up with a plan to try and save her life. She brought her to our yard and released her, hoping that she may be able to live out her days as she did before – as a feral cat. Thankfully, it seemed that the plan was going better than expected, as Tinkerbell was growing in confidence day by day.

Solitary cat

As the months progressed, Tinkerbell was beginning to show a very clear liking to Lauren, and she was starting to trust her more and more. She was now starting to copy Teddy, and she was rubbing against our legs and enjoying a stroke, although understandably it had to be on her terms. It was lovely to see how Teddy was looking after her, and many a day we found them curled up together.

But then a slight bombshell hit. Teddy, from the first day he appeared, had made it very clear which person he favoured, and he had worked his charms on this lady to such an extent that she wanted to take him home with her. The cold winter we were experiencing had made her feel very concerned about his welfare, and we all agreed with her that for a domestic cat it was a harsh way of life. Teddy needed his home comforts.

So Teddy went on to live a wonderful life with the woman who adored him. And her feelings were totally reciprocated, because Teddy went on to become her shadow. She often said that in his love and adoration for her, he was acting more like a dog than a cat.

Although it was totally the right thing for Teddy to live out the rest of his life in comfort and warmth, we did still worry about how Tinkerbell would cope losing her friend. But to all intents and purposes she seemed fine with it, and she continued to seek out contact and affection from us.

Animal Communication reading

About a year after we had first laid eyes on Tinky, we asked the lady who had carried out an Animal

Communication on Tiffany if she would please carry out a communication on Tinky. This would be the lady who I would eventually do my Animal Communication training with.

At the time of the reading, I was starting to feel that Tinky may be brave enough to sit on our laps. It really felt like she was trying to build up the confidence to do this, and I had a strong feeling that it may not be too long before she achieved it. Interestingly, in the reading, Tinky did make reference to the fact that she was building up the courage to sit on our laps. I knew it was going to happen; and soon!

She also brought up the sadness she had felt about losing her kittens. Yes, the pain of this must have been awful for her. It was easy to associate with her pain.

Reiki cat

Not long after the reading, Tinky did indeed sit on Lauren's lap. It was an incredibly joyful moment. We applauded her courage and how far she had come. Every day she was getting more trusting.

Although there were a few of us on the yard who were feeding her, I have to say that Lauren was her clear favourite, and the person she trusted the most. She began to let Lauren pick her up and carry her around, and she was the only person on the yard who she would allow to do this to her.

Although not as loved as Lauren, I did come a close second! I am convinced that the Reiki on offer helped her to start trusting me, as she did absolutely love her Reiki sessions. I would sit down and she would jump on to my lap. As the Reiki started to flow, she would purr and drool, and she would happily stay like that for ages. Eventually, through lack of time, I would be forced to bring the session to an end, and encourage her gently back onto her feet, but I would always feel bad that I couldn't continue it for longer, as she clearly absolutely loved these sessions. It was just wonderful to hear her purring madly away, but not so pleasurable having to clean myself of drool.

Then came the time when on the odd occasion, Tinky would climb up my back and sit on my shoulder. I was simply amazed by this. How could a cat who was once so terrified and distrustful of people become this tame? It just seemed incredible that Tinky had learned to trust us this much.

Interestingly, although others on the yard fed her, she was much more wary of other people. It was Lauren and I who she had singled out to be her family. Then one day, my dad came up the yard, and I was absolutely astonished that she reacted to him with the same calmness and trust that she did with us. She was quite happy for him to stroke and fuss her. It seemed that she recognised he was my dad, and as a result she was able to extend her trust to this new member of kin.

Health problems

When Tinky had been rescued, they aged her about seven years old. So she was young, but sadly she was not intended for a long life.

It was obvious from very early on that she seemed to have a mouth issue. Every so often she would let out a little scream and run around while contorting her mouth.

Tinky was about to deliver a very powerful lesson to us. And the lesson was this: it is not for us to try and control another's life. Sometimes, you just have to respect an animal's wishes, and Tinky's wishes were very clear. On no account did she want to be put in a pet carrier and taken to the vets.

The number of times I arranged a vet visit for her, only to find that it was impossible to get her into a cat carrier. We tried everything – picking her up and trying to force her in, leaving a carrier up the yard with food in it, using bribery to get her in, and trying to relax her with Reiki before attempting to put her in, but it was all to no avail. She was having none of it! I guess the carrier was just a reminder of her entrapment, and she was not going to ever allow herself to be constricted in that way again. To be fair to her, although she was a fairly small cat, her gentleness always meant that although she struggled and leaped out of our arms, she never resorted to biting or scratching. She really was the gentlest of cats, and we loved her for it.

We always worried that these attempts at entrapment would cause her to lose trust in us. But thankfully, it never did! She would hide and lick her wounds for a few hours, and then she would carry on like nothing had ever happened.

She had been at the yard possibly about three years, when it was clear that her health was deteriorating. She had stopped cleaning herself, and her eating which had always been a bit erratic (possibly because of her mouth problems), had become increasingly so. She was starting to lose a lot of weight.

Attempts to get her to a vet continued to be futile. There were a lot of experienced cat owners at the yard, but nobody was able to come up with a successful plan of getting her to the vets.

In my heart of hearts, I knew that it was Tinky's decision not to be treated, and that her soul had chosen a relatively short life. Maybe she had accomplished everything in this life that she had intended to, and it was now her time to go home. Somehow, we had to make peace with what was to be Tinky's choice.

The last goodbye

I was crouched on the ground picking out Jazz's feet, when I was startled by a cat running and jumping into my lap. I let out a small scream, frightening poor Tinky in the process. And that was the last time that I would lay eyes on her.

It was so sad that my last contact with Tinky was one where I frightened her and she ran off. If only it had been a loving last encounter, where she was sitting on my lap, drooling all over me (oh, how I miss that drool!).

After a couple of days of not seeing Tinky, I tried using Animal Communication to connect with her, and it became immediately obvious that she had passed into the light. I could sense her soul was at peace. I don't know the circumstances of her death because she didn't want to show me, as she felt it wasn't in my interest or for my highest good to know such a thing. Both Lauren and I cried our eyes out when we realised that we wouldn't see her again. She was such a gentle, loving friend, and for her to have put her trust in us like she had was a beautiful gift indeed. We felt empty and bereft without her. Who would have thought that a cat, once so feral, could have left such a hole in our lives?

I always believe that things happen for a reason. Some of you reading this may feel that we should have done more to have saved her life. But I do think it is very important to respect another person's/animal's wishes. I absolutely believe 100% that we do not die, we transition into another life, and I also believe that our soul plans its departure before coming to Earth; or at the very least, it plans opportunities for its exit if it should so choose.

Now, six years on, I realise how difficult things would have been if she had continued to live. For the person who lived at the yard became engaged. The lady who came to live with him had dogs, and she would not allow cats on the yard. Another cat who arrived about a year or two after Tinky was very quickly sent on his way, and very strict instructions were issued to the effect that cats were no longer tolerated or allowed on the yard.

Then, not long after, we moved Jazz to another yard. So Tinky's fate would have been quite grim and I dread to think what would have become of her. I know she would never have tolerated being a house cat, as she could not cope with having doors closed on her. She valued her freedom way too much to be cooped up anywhere.

So although one of Tinky's lessons for us was one of patience, the biggest one was respecting another Being's wishes and trusting that the unfolding of another's life and physical transition was happening in the way it was intended. Not everyone is expected to live a long physical life. Clearly Tinky had completed everything she needed to do here and she was ready to go home.

It is human nature to want to try and control things and outcomes, but sometimes it is much better to go with the flow. To let go and let be, accepting what is. This is a very important lesson for us Humans, and it is a lesson that Tinky passed on to us.

Until Tinky entered our lives, I had never really experienced a close connection with a cat. But she changed that, and I will be forever grateful for the friendship we shared, and the beautiful Reiki sessions we enjoyed together. I am also indebted to her for the joy she planted in Lauren – for there is nothing quite as fulfilling as winning the trust of what was once a feral animal. Their bond and love for each other was truly beautiful to witness, and by marking Lauren out as "the special one" she had really helped boost her self-confidence and self-esteem during those early teenage years.

It seems most appropriate that Lauren has now become a small animal vet, and has recently taken on two kittens from The Cat Sanctuary. I am sure that Tinky is watching over her with great pride at her accomplishments, knowing that she had a huge part to play in Lauren's love of cats.

A self-reflection exercise

- Give yourself time to reflect, making sure there are no distractions and you won't be disturbed.

- Start to connect to your breath, taking deep breaths in through the nose, and out through the mouth.

- When you are fully relaxed, think about a time in your life when you utilised great patience. Really engage with this experience and imagine yourself in that situation again. Think of the benefits to your life, and the gifts you received from having such patience.

Our society is very much about getting what we want when we want, but in actual fact this doesn't serve us at all, as we just become ungracious and take everything for granted. When you have to wait for something, you appreciate it far more when it comes into your life. Your gratitude overflows, and it is this energy which helps to lift you up. The rewards for patience are just enormous!

- When you have connected to the feelings of gratitude, reflect on the relationship with an animal in your life. Where could you adopt more patience? Think about the changes you could make which will help support your animal. Having patience often means breaking things down into smaller chunks when we are dealing with our animals, so consider how you could assist them by taking things at a slower pace. Having patience also means that sometimes we have to rewind and take a step backwards if our animal has given signs that we have overstepped the mark.

Just remember, it is so important when dealing with animals to offer them our patience and understanding. Often, we have to step out of our human perceptions, and see things from the animal's viewpoint. Their idea of what is right for them, may be very different to our own, and somewhere along the trajectory, we have to try and marry the two!

PART 3 – ANIMALS AS SENTIENT BEINGS

What sort of ignorance denies the sentience of animals?
The same sort that has brought the world to the state of collapse.
When we recognise, honour and appreciate that animal's gifts to Humans
Go way beyond using their bodies for our own ends.
Then we can start building a world where we can all thrive.

When the sentience of animals was finally declared as being fact in 2022, I could barely believe it. Not because I was questioning the truth of the claim, but that it had taken so long for scientists to officially recognise such a thing. In one respect, with our technological advances, we seem so advanced, and yet in other areas of life we seem so backward that we could even be described as positively primitive.

I had no doubt of animal's sentience, even as early as age four. And I hadn't even had much experience around animals at that point. But something did happen at that age which enabled me to feel the deep pain and fear that animals can be privy to. The dog who initiated me into these deep depths of emotion had been abandoned and was hanging loose around the neighbourhood. He was a big dog, and so for young children who were not used to dogs, he may have seemed a bit intimidating. Not so for my friend and I. We befriended him, and enjoyed hanging out with him, until the day came when he was rounded up and taken away, presumably by the RSPCA.

I can still conjure up the feelings of fear and deep distress that I was feeling on behalf of that dog. For a young child who was growing up in a happy, loving and secure home, these deep emotions were very new. There was no denying that I was really feeling and experiencing this dog's pain and fear. It was also the first time that I realised not everyone has a loving home. Abandoning an animal was truly shocking to me, and when my parents explained what was happening to this dog, I could barely get my head around it. How could anyone just throw a defenceless animal on to the streets? My heart was breaking that humans could do such a thing. The fact that I am recalling it now, over fifty years later, gives you an idea of how affected I was by the whole thing.

Ten years on from this, I would come across another abandoned dog; a puppy sitting in the middle of a field, shaking and looking distraught. As I looked down at this puppy, her eyes bore deep into my own. She held my gaze for about twenty seconds, and in that time, she told me everything I needed to know. As long as I live, I will never forget that dog's plea for help. She touched my soul and left me deeply affected. As well as pleading with me to help her, she was also passing on information. She told me that she had been taken there by car and dumped. I had no idea at the time that this was Animal Communication at its very best; a direct message passing from one soul in need to another soul who could help.

Having received this dog's heartfelt message, there was only one thing left to do. I picked her up in my arms and reassured her that I would help find her a home. I would do everything in my power to help her.

The moment I placed her back on the ground, she was a changed dog. There was no denying she had understood my promise to help her. She bounded around me in joyful abandon like we had been together forever, and she accompanied me all the way to the yard to do my horse duties and then all the way back home.

I so wanted to keep her, but sadly, our dog made it very clear that she was not going to tolerate another dog in the house (years later, she would apologise for this – see the chapter on Candy). Thankfully, a friend came to the rescue and they took in this beautiful mongrel puppy who they named Ellie. She went on to live a full and happy life, although her wounds of abandonment did remain with her, and she always stuck like glue to her Guardians whenever they walked her. This just shows how deeply emotions run in our animals, and it is something our world really needs to recognise. Animals aren't just toys to play with when the need arises. They are sensitive, heartfelt Beings, who feel emotions as deeply as we do and who are wounded in much the same way as us.

As is so revealing in these stories, when it comes to overcoming challenges in life, animals aren't really so different from ourselves. Their emotions can be just as complex and affecting as our own.

We applaud animals for living in the "now" and assume that because of this, they don't have the hang-ups we have, resulting from living in the past, or dreaming of the future. Animals, it is claimed, live well and truly in the present moment.

Although this is true to a certain extent, it doesn't mean to say that they aren't deeply wounded by events that life has thrown their way, and their behaviours can be affected as a result.

As you will see, when you come to read about the animals in the next few chapters, they do seem to exhibit almost human reactions to their dilemmas and situations. In Annie's story we are witness to the same trauma we exhibit when we come face to face with a traumatic health diagnosis - the stages of anger, denial, depression and finally acceptance are not just emotions we experience, but are felt just as keenly by our animals.

Most people don't believe that animals can feel the emotion of guilt, but Prince's story really does throw this thinking into the fire. His story also demonstrates beautifully the highs and lows of being highly empathic. It isn't just humans who struggle with having an empathic nature!

We are asked to consider the role of ego in Rosie's story. Do we let our ego get in the way of seeing animals for who they truly are?

Finally, Ivor provides a bit of humour in his story, as we learn that animals too can believe they have been born into the wrong body.

After reading their stories, it is impossible to deny that just like us, animals can be highly empathic and intuitive, exhibiting reactions of heightened sensitivity to what is happening around them, whether that be denial of a physical diagnosis, feeling guilt for a misdemeanour, feeling like their sentience is not being recognised, or even feeling like they have been born into the wrong body.

Like us, animals respond extremely well to empathy, understanding and compassion, and this is where healing modalities like Reiki healing are so very helpful in allowing these animals to find acceptance and healing. We all have a deep desire to be understood, and animals are no different in requiring this deep need to be met. In the following chapters you will read about how effective Reiki healing can be in helping animals overcome their deep rooted, emotional pain. They weren't the only ones though to benefit. In helping them, they also had a lot to teach me.

ANNIE

A Lesson in Acceptance

*We have been taught that will is everything
Only hard work, stubbornness and determination
Will make our dreams come alive.
But the Universe always knows best
And when we let go
The energies of the Universe will flow,
Bringing forth a blessing
The ego mind could never comprehend.*

Annie is a horse for whom I will always have a huge debt of gratitude towards. She was very special in many ways, and she is a horse I became acquainted with a couple of years before losing Tiffany.

She was a stunning thoroughbred mare. In her younger days, she had been a competition horse, but Della bought her with the intention of hacking and low level competing. More than anything, it was hoped they could have many happy years together.

I was on the same yard as Della, and she very generously let me ride Annie from time to time. Annie was a wonderful horse to ride. She was kind, spirited and very forgiving, and with her beautiful movement and floating paces, riding her was quite the experience.

One instance particularly stands out in my memory. Della had gone on a two week holiday, and she had entrusted her to my care. I tried to make the most of the experience, exercising Annie as much as possible. But the highlight of the two weeks, was taking her on a fun ride, accompanying my daughter and her friend on their ponies. Wow, what a ride that turned out to be! Annie was just incredible that day, and no horse could have given more of themselves.

Annie was an exciting horse to ride at the best of times, but this particular day will always be remembered as being one of the greatest rides of my life. Exuding lightness of energy, Annie was an absolute dream for the whole of the ride. She was light in my hand, light off my leg, and even though I hadn't jumped in a long time, she carried me effortlessly over many jumps, calmly waiting on the other side, while the kids caught up and jumped the smaller jumps with their ponies. My gratitude for what she had gifted me that special day actually had me in tears. I was just blown away by her!

In the ensuing years, I was able to repay part of my debt to her, although what she had blessed me with that day far exceeded my paltry offerings.

The torn stifle

A year or two after my magical ride, when Annie was 17 years old, she tore her stifle (corresponds to knee joint in humans). It took about three months for a diagnosis to be made, and when it was, the prognosis wasn't great. The vets wanted her to be stabled for a three month period, but for a horse as spirited as Annie, this was never going to be an easy task. Stabling any horse for 24 hours a day can take a huge toll on their emotional/mental state, but with a horse as energetic as Annie, it was almost asking the impossible.

Even with the stable rest, the vet was apprehensive as to how successful it would be. Offering only 50% chance of success, Della decided it would be more than her horse could deal with. So instead, she erected a small paddock in the field, hoping that this would be enough to keep Annie mentally calm, as well as giving the tear a good chance to heal.

Sadly as feared, Annie was not at all happy with this arrangement, and she was becoming increasingly difficult to handle. Della was struggling to lead her calmly from paddock to stable, and vice versa, and she was spending a lot of time, rearing, bucking and galloping around the field. I sensed that she was really angry with the diagnosis, as she was a horse who had always loved her work. She loved to be mentally stimulated and able to utilise her energy, so this arrangement was just very difficult for her.

Reiki Healing

It had entered my awareness that Annie was a horse who responded really well to Reiki energy.

There had been an evening when I had been carrying out some self-reiki before venturing up the yard. As a result, I was feeling particularly calm and blissed out. Arriving on the yard, I was witness to Della attempting to lead an adrenaline fuelled Annie across the yard. As she drew next to me, Annie on two legs, I just happened to draw a long breath and place my hands on Annie's body. The effect was instantaneous. The speed her energy dissipated was reminiscent of the speed a balloon deflates when you pop it. She instantly calmed, and walked into her stable as quiet as a lamb.

Her reaction told me all I needed to know. Annie would be a great Reiki candidate.

At this point in my life, I had just been attuned to Reiki 2, and I needed a few case studies to practise on. Putting my lack of confidence aside, I decided to ask Della if she would agree to Annie being one of my case studies. Thankfully, she happily agreed.

Like all newly attuned Reiki graduates, I entered this arrangement with only one thought in my mind. Come rain or shine, Annie was going to be healed, and I was going to be the one who would make the difference. Boy, did I have a lot to learn! Annie was going to deliver me a hard and difficult lesson.

The first session

The first session with Annie was very uplifting. As expected, she just loved and responded really well to the Reiki energy.

For ten minutes, I just worked on her injured back leg. She stood in the middle of the stable, sighing, licking and chewing and was quite happy for me to do the work. After I finished, Annie rubbed her head up me, as if saying thank you.

I impressed on her the need for her to be calm, explaining that her leg would never heal if she carried on cavorting around.

The next day I carried out the same routine. She was quite accepting and just carried on eating.

I carried out small healing sessions on her for the next seven days. As expected, she absolutely loved it, and would try so hard to give something back. This normally consisted of her trying to groom me, and in some sessions she would spend the whole time sucking on the end of my boot.

Emotionally, Annie responded really well. From the first day of Reiki, she calmed down completely. The mad careering around the field ceased, and she became easy to lead in and out. Typically, when we used to lead our horses past her, her normal reaction was to charge at the fence with her ears back. But since the first day of healing, she hadn't done this once. There was no doubt about it. Annie was feeling much happier.

Despite the emotional changes, Annie's leg was no better and the trot trials that were carried out indicated that it had worsened. I felt completely disillusioned and concerned that I had given Della false hope. My confidence was shattered!

Due to a lot happening in my life, I didn't carry out any healing for three months. In this time, the vet had made it clear that she should be retired and put on Bute (a painkiller) and there was talk about her being put to sleep. At these times, Annie had become very depressed – she didn't want Della to lose hope.

I felt her sadness. In her previous home she had just been used as a competition horse, and her personality and character had been cast aside. In fact, Della had been informed by the previous owner that she wasn't an affectionate horse at all and was very aloof, but this wasn't true at all. On the contrary, Annie was a really engaging and sweet horse. She was now in a home where her worth was fully recognised, and she wanted to give her best to this woman who valued her so highly. How difficult for her, that now she had found the perfect home, her injury was threatening their wonderful life together. It seemed a cruel twist of fate!

Requesting Reiki

Then something amazing happened. Annie would tell me when she needed a Reiki session.

I would be walking past her field, and she would whinny to me and come over. I would go in the field and offer her Reiki, and always she would choose to take it. The sessions were always beautiful, peaceful and comforting. I was starting to hear the words "*Peace*" and "*Acceptance*" which made me think this was what Annie was taking away from the Reiki. It appeared to be really helping her to come to terms with her injury.

The wounded healer

Around this time, I decided to pull a card from my "Way of the Horse" cards (Linda Kohanav). What could they tell me about what was going on with Annie?

Amazingly, the card I pulled out was Chiron – the wounded healer. I found it fascinating that Chiron's knee was wounded through a poisoned arrow, and in attempting to heal it, he discovered the healing arts. Somehow, this seemed to be a parallel with what was happening to Annie. As well as the injured leg, I could relate to her as a healer, recalling the time when we were in the barn with her and Lauren was doubled over with stomach ache. Annie had stood over her, putting her head in Lauren's lap and leaving it there for a few minutes until Lauren felt a lot better. We were both awed at the empathy shown.

The information for the card stated *"A deeper integration of body, mind, and spirit sometimes emerges through an accident or illness. Healing requires accessing the wisdom behind the wound."* It also explained that the wounded healer archetype lives in the horses themselves. Instead of viewing them as victims, we should recognise them as sentient beings with a destiny of their own.

I felt that the message for me was to stop seeing Annie as a victim. My obsession with the physical healing of the leg had been my ego mind running the show, but I was now being asked to step back from this and see the bigger picture. Was there something else at play here? Annie had lessons to learn in life the same as I did, and maybe this whole episode was part of Annie's destiny and her soul contract. Maybe her soul had planned for this to happen, and possibly it was her planned exit out of the physical body.

My reflection on why this card had shown itself was a game changer for me. I now recognised that I needed to let Reiki do its work and to stop trying to force the outcome my ego mind desired. We were working at the soul level here, and I needed to release the outcome and let it go. A big part of Reiki is to trust it will go where it is most needed, which is a very different thing to trying to force it to go where we think it is needed. The two just don't correlate!

Transition

I continued to give Annie Reiki when she asked for it.

Sadly, her leg never healed and the decision was finally made to put her to sleep. By this stage, whenever I carried out Reiki on Annie, the words *"Peace"* and *"Acceptance"* would crescendo around my head. I was beginning to recognise that this was why Annie loved the Reiki so much. It was helping her to come to terms with her fate; the decision she had made before coming to Earth. This was her planned exit, but being in a physical body, and with an ego mind, she still needed to make peace with it.

The day of her transition, she was a model of peace and acceptance. She quietly and calmly acquiesced to what was asked of her, and she gracefully lifted out of her physical body.

Knowing whether it is the right time to assist an animal in the dying process is something that all animal lovers have to grapple with at some point. It is without doubt the worst thing about loving and owning an animal. It tears at our conscience. Do we keep them alive, even though they are suffering, or do we help to quicken their demise? People are so divided by this, and so many people let guilt get the better of them. Did they keep their animal alive for too long, prolonging their suffering, or did they end their life too soon? So many people agonise over their decision, yet the truth as I see it is that there is no right or wrong. Our animals know when they pass over that we only had their best interests in mind, and they will only ever love us for caring so much and for making these tough decisions on their behalf. The soul is eternal and death is an illusion, so in the great scheme of things it matters not a jot.

My teaching

Although my ego mind was massively disappointed that I hadn't succeeded in helping Annie to heal physically, I also recognised that it had been a huge lesson for me in the art of Reiki.

A big part of using Reiki is to let go of the outcome. With Annie, it had become increasingly clear that she needed the Reiki healing to help her accept her fate and to make peace with it. And in this respect, the Reiki had been hugely successful.

In the ensuing years, I have discovered the gift in letting go of outcomes. It is human nature to try and make things happen through force, wilfulness, hard work and sheer stubbornness, but by forcing things, we may be missing out on something much more beneficial and rewarding for us. If there was a tree blocking the road, you would look for an alternative way around it. Yet when we come across blocks and setbacks in life, we just want to plough straight through them.

It is at these times you need to pause and ask yourself if the Universe is trying to tell you something, because there is a really strong possibility that you are being redirected onto a different path. In time, it becomes easier to recognise these roadblocks, and to consider alternative possibilities. I liken this to flowing with the Universe. I can only speak from my own viewpoint, but taking the time to consider where I am being led (by the Universe) has helped me enormously on my life journey, bringing me much needed peace and fulfilment in the process.

A self-reflection exercise

- Give yourself time to reflect, making sure there are no distractions and you won't be disturbed.

- Start to connect to your breath, taking deep breaths in through the nose, and out through the mouth.

- When you are fully relaxed, ask yourself the question, *"Is there anything in my life that I am trying to force or make happen?"*

- Take the first thing that comes up for you.

- Think deeply about the situation that has come up, and try standing back from it and looking at it from an outsider point of view. Consider that this may not be the right thing for you, or maybe a different perspective is required. Think about the different ways it could be viewed, and also consider whether it may be worth stepping back from and allowing something better to come in.

- You could try connecting to your higher self and asking it to show you a better course of action. Whatever comes up, trust it, and promise yourself that you will give it a go. You may be surprised at what materialises.

Just remember, things are never black or white, and sometimes we have to step away from our logical mind to see things differently. If I am really undecided on a course of action, I will ask my pendulum, or I will consult my oracle cards. I do this because more often than not they give me a perspective that I may not have considered and it really helps me to take this into consideration when moving forwards. It is a wonderful way to navigate life!

When you change the way you look at something, the resulting picture can be very different indeed. This is the road to peace!

PRINCE

A Lesson in Trust and Non-Judgement

I am not my bad behaviour.
When I behave out of character
It is just a reflection of my insecurities
Ignited by my fears
But it is not who I am.
Please take the time to see the real me.

Prince is a horse who will always hold a special place in my heart. He was never my horse or even close to being my horse, but he was prepared to share some of his special soul with me, and for that I will always be grateful. Through Prince, I also learned some beneficial lessons. I learned the huge benefits of building a relationship based on trust, and how when this is established everything else becomes much easier. Additionally, a powerful lesson on non-judgement was to be delivered to me.

Prince was bought by a couple for their grand-daughter, Becky. They were a wonderful family, and with them, Prince was in really loving hands.

For a while they had Prince on the same yard as my horse Jazz, and it was where I first met him. He was a beautiful grey seven year old 15.2hh Irish Sports horse, but he seemed much bigger than that. On the surface, he appeared solid, kind, dependable, with an endearing personality, and it was for these reasons they had bought him a couple of years before as an ideal and safe horse for Becky.

Becky needed a safe horse because she had undergone scoliosis surgery. The specialist had warned that if she had a fall then it would dislodge all the metal plates in her back, meaning that another major operation would be necessary. So Prince was considered the safe horse that Becky needed, and they had bought him about a year before I met them.

But appearances can be deceptive, for, as I became acquainted with Prince, I was to discover that he was a deeply sensitive, sometimes fearful horse, and he was hugely empathic - just how much so was proven in a remarkable incident.

Incredible Intuition

It was a beautiful summer evening, and Prince's owners were busy mucking out his field. As I walked past them, I was mystified as to why Prince kept looking up and neighing. He was directing his attention to fields which were about 200 feet away. Between him and these fields was a 60 foot menage, a bank and some hedging, so it was impossible to see what he was neighing at.

He stopped grazing completely and his neighing became more incessant. It was like he was trying to alert our attention to something. About ten minutes of this, someone ventured along that path to fetch their horse in, and discovered one of the ponies rolling about in agony with colic. This pony was a friend of Prince's, and even though he couldn't see her from his own field, and he was quite a distance away, he had just known she was in trouble.

Maisie the pony was hurriedly fetched out the field, brought into the stable, and the vet was called. Prince continued to neigh to her. Such was his concern, that someone very kindly agreed to swap stables so he could be next to her. I can still picture him, watching her through the bars of the stable, his empathic concern so much in evidence.

Thankfully, Maisie was fine, and proceeded to make a good recovery, none the worst for her ordeal. But for those of us who had witnessed it, we were just gobsmacked by the whole event – not just the empathy and concern shown towards his friend, but the fact he knew something was seriously wrong. How had he known? His sixth sense had clearly been working overtime. Anyone doubting that horses' could be this intuitive, really needed to experience this event to believe it.

Prince had proven emphatically that he had a huge and beautiful heart.

A need for healing

Just as with people, sensitive and empathic animals can have more difficulties in life than animals who don't have these qualities. And Prince was no exception to this rule!

I was originally sought out by his Guardians to see if I could possibly help with his clipping issues. A lady had come to the yard to carry out a job of clipping a few horses, Prince being one of them, but he had reacted very badly to the noise of the clippers.

In order to gain Prince's trust, before I did anything with him, I decided to carry out an Animal Communication to try and get to the heart of the problem. He showed me how force had been used in the past (not with his current Guardians), and I could see a lot of smacking and shouting taking place. Just the noise of the clippers would trigger these memories and create a lot of anxiety for him.

After the Animal Communication, I carried out some Reiki healing in the stable with him as a means of releasing any past trauma. The session was quite incredible, as it really connected me with Prince on the soul level, and I actually received a great deal of healing myself. It was one of those occasions when I was wondering who was healing who, because I genuinely believe that this empathic, loving horse was doing more for me than I was for him. I still have my notes from that session, and I set out some excerpts from it below:-

REIKI SESSION – 13 OCTOBER 2017

I decided that tonight was the right time to go up the yard and carry out a Reiki session on Prince, as not only would it be quiet, but it was also a lovely warm evening. I arrived at 7.15pm and everyone was leaving or had left, so it was very peaceful.

I grounded myself and connected to Source, calling in my spiritual helpers. I entered Prince's stable and asked him if he was happy to receive some Reiki. He responded positively, sniffing the energy in my hands. I asked him to direct me where he wanted the energy to go.

To start with, he was very keen to push his nose into my hands and to lick me. He was also enjoying rubbing his nose on my hands, and he was making funny crinkly movements with it – very different to anything I have seen a horse do before. I have found with animals that I have carried out an Animal Communication with beforehand, that a connection already seems to be formed with them. And when they see me in person, they always want to lick or kiss me. This seems to be their way of thanking me and showing appreciation for the help I am giving them.

After about ten minutes, Prince moves his body slightly, allowing me to put my hands on his Brachial chakra. Almost straight away, he let out a really strange noise – like a sigh and a grunt combined. I take this as a sign that he is releasing something. In the whole session, he made this noise about seven times. I move my hands to his back and place my hands on his solar plexus and sacral chakra. He is happy with this, but not so happy when I attempt to put my hands on his root chakra. He puts his ears back slightly and starts to paw with his front feet. I move back to his shoulder, as I don't want to force anything on him.

Prince starts to eat his hay. I feel the impulse to put my left hand on his heart, and my right, on the brachial chakra. We continue like this for about ten minutes. I decide to scan his aura. Everything feels normal, apart from the root chakra. My fingers are really pulsating as I hold them above this area. I guess with his fear issues, and his dislike of having things forced on him, it is not surprising that this chakra feels blocked. He is now happy for me to work on this area, so I do until my fingers stop tingling.

I feel the urge to put my hands just under his throat (not touching) on both sides. Almost immediately he makes that strange sigh/grunt noise, quickly followed by a repeat of that noise. There is clearly some releasing going on here.

I feel that it is time for the session to come to an end. As I thank him for his cooperation, he promptly starts licking me again. He starts to get sleepy, and he rests his muzzle on my left hand, while I place my right hand over his third eye. We remain like this for about ten minutes. I feel a very strong connection to Prince's spirit, and he takes me to a really beautiful place; a place where I feel humbled by the horse's generous and gentle spirit. In this reverie, I feel our minds merging, and a deep sense of calm and peace takes over. I feel he is healing me, as much as I am healing him. In this state, I wonder why we don't spend more time just hanging out with our horses.

I thank Prince for allowing me to work with him, and for the deep inner peace he has passed on to me. I sweep his aura and ask for anything to be taken away that does not belong to Prince, and to give Prince back anything that does belong to him. I clear myself and disconnect from his energy.

I feel it has been a very productive session. Not just for Prince, but for me also. We have both benefitted from the healing energy.

SHAVER TRAINING

Following the Reiki session, I took a shaver up the yard, and for about 5 or 10 minutes a night, I approached Prince in his stable with the shaver running. To start with he was very tense, and I stayed outside the stable with it.

After only about four very short sessions, he was happy for me to enter his stable with it, and happy to lick me with his face very close to the shaver. After a few nights of this, he was happy for me to touch his body with it, while I scratched his withers, although he did remain tense. Whenever he showed resistance, backing away, I would retreat and let him come to me.

About a week of this and there was a real breakthrough. He was sleeping at the back of his stable, when I turned the shaver on, about 20 feet away. He woke up, pricked his ears and put his head over the door. This was great because he was showing signs of having good associations with it.

I approached him and entered his stable. Although I had not connected to Reiki and had not intended a Reiki session, I was starting to feel a lot of Reiki energy coming through my left hand which was holding the shaver. As I felt this, Prince started to yawn, lick and chew. I turned the shaver off and put my right hand on the brachial chakra and the left on his shoulder. Prince instantly became very still, standing like a statue, with me at the side of him, but the stance was very relaxed, with no tension whatsoever. I felt a lovely calm energy wrap around us. We stood in that beautiful stillness for about five minutes until someone came over to chat. Prince peeled back his lips, like he had tasted something funny, then he started eating his hay.

This all felt very positive and I received the impression that Prince had shed another layer of fear. What I would go on to discover is that this work I carried out with him, would help us bond on a level where his trust in me would help with some of his other issues. But before this, Prince was going to hurt someone very badly.

The accident

It is always important to consider when someone behaves badly, what exactly lies behind that behaviour. This applies to people and animals. It is very easy to judge and condemn, but less easy to understand and have compassion. Yet, always there is a reason.

This is why Prince's story is so important. You can have the most beautiful soul, in possession of the biggest heart possible, but it still doesn't mean that at some point in their life, they are not going to behave badly. In the case of animals, bad behaviour is pretty well always a result of pain, fear, or emotional overload.

It was around March 2018 when a horrific accident occurred, and Prince was at the heart of it.

Although he was bought as a very safe hack, in more recent times Prince had developed some insecurities about being hacked out. So much so, that Becky was only riding him in the menage. An instructor was paid to hack him out and also to school him. One day, she had a battle with Prince over opening and closing a gate. There was some force applied to him, and being the sensitive horse he is, he reacted quite badly to her forceful, angry attitude. He didn't throw her, but he scared her enough for her to state quite emphatically to the family that in her opinion he was too dangerous for Becky to ride.

So another instructor was found. She was a lovely young lady and she seemed perfect for Prince – gentle, kind, compassionate and understanding, Like the rest of us, she could see straight through to his beautiful heart.

But at his saddle check fitting a few months later, something had gone wrong between them. Although he had been fine for Becky, he had thrown the instructor off, before careering around the menage. It was really strange, and those who had witnessed it were struggling to understand why he had done it. The only explanation was that he had lifted more at the withers for the instructor, and so had possibly experienced some back pain, or some physical discomfort. I later tuned into him and felt some back pain, with a saddle that wasn't quite right for him, so this was a possible explanation.

The next day, the instructor had arranged to ride him out with me on my horse Jazz. When I heard about her fall, I questioned whether riding out was the best course of action. She reassured me that it was fine and she wanted to proceed, but her body language was telling me differently. And Prince could sense it too, because he was quite averse to her getting on his back. I wish so much that I could have talked her out of it, but as they say, hindsight is a wonderful thing.

We set off, Jazz in front and Prince behind. We walked a small distance down the road, then turned into a field where we proceeded to ride around the edge. That's when everything went wrong and Prince completely lost the plot. As we walked quietly, he suddenly came charging past Jazz, bucking whilst doing so. Although the instructor was an excellent rider, she had no chance of staying on. Following her fall, Prince galloped up and down the field, bucking and rearing like something possessed. He then galloped home, narrowly missing colliding with a car.

I really don't like to dwell on it, because it haunted me for years, but the poor instructor had broken her back, although thankfully she did go on to make a full recovery. Nevertheless, it was a horrendous experience for her, and left her with months of lying in a bed.

We were all badly affected by that accident. I had to carry out Reiki on my horse Jazz, and it would be months before I felt comfortable to hack out again. At the same time, this was nothing compared to what the instructor had suffered.

Then there was Prince himself. He was suddenly considered a pariah, and desperate attempts were made to convince his Guardians that they should sell him, as he was completely mad and unsafe. Being the empath he was, he was feeling all these emotions that everyone was directing at him, and it was making him thoroughly miserable.

Even though I had experienced those beautiful connections with him, I felt furious with him too, and so angry that he had hurt my friend.

But the saving grace for Prince was that he had such amazing Guardians who loved him dearly. Although heartbroken at what had happened, they were determined to stand by him and help him through it. For yes, he too needed healing.

Guilt

Just days after the accident, his family asked me if I would please carry out some Reiki on Prince. He was utterly depressed, miserable and feeling guilty. So much so, that when they tried to comfort him, he would just turn away from them like he felt he didn't deserve their sympathy. He had always been an incredibly loving horse, lapping up fuss and attention, but now he just didn't feel like he deserved it. He was utterly dejected and it was breaking his family's hearts.

I am so glad they asked me to carry out some Reiki on him, because it really helped me heal my own anger towards him. For when I felt into why he had behaved this way, I was able to see things from his perspective.

The knowledge I gleaned was that he had felt some pain from the saddle the day before, but the main reason was that he was picking up on the instructor's own anxiety about riding him. Being so empathic, he would have taken on her fears and anxieties as his own, until he became a pressure cooker that exploded. I knew he hadn't meant her any serious harm. He just wanted to be free of her anxiety that was fuelling his own. And this is the thing with animals. They will react to pain or fear in the moment, but their brains don't work the same as ours, and so they are unable to think through the possible consequences of their actions.

The Reiki I carried out on Prince was instantly successful. He was able to release his guilt and anxiety, allowing him to revert back to his normal, loving self.

Lunging

It was decided that it may be best to lunge Prince, and just allow Becky to ride him in the menage; for the time being anyway.

His family asked if I would possibly do a little lunging with him, and I happily agreed. There was also another challenge to overcome. Prince was absolutely terrified of the long lunge whip – so much so, that once when the first instructor was lunging him, he got loose and jumped the five bar gate out of the school, bringing it down in the process.

To start with I carried out some very gentle groundwork with him, and I would just pick up the whip, let him sniff it and then put it down again. After a few sessions, he was totally comfortable with it, and we had progressed to him being happy with me stroking him all over with it.

Henceforth, it took very little effort for him to be happy about lunging with it.

Prince was a wonderful candidate for the lunge work. He understood my requests very easily, and the lunge whip was only needed to keep him out on the circle and not to fall in, but following the gentle introduction with the whip, it was never a problem for him. The lunging really helped to teach him to balance himself, and because of it, his riding work with Becky had become so much more effortless.

Again, I felt the Animal Communication and Reiki work we had done, had established a trust between us that made his improvements occur effortlessly.

Transport loading

Transport loading was another big fear of Prince's; understandably, as he had undergone a long journey from Ireland to the West Midlands. Added to which there had been an incident where he had straddled the breast-bar in the trailer.

It was no wonder that Prince disliked the trailer so much. But we needed to change his feelings about it, as a move to a new yard was on the cards, and he would need to travel in order to get there. Another opportunity to help Prince had presented itself.

I had never seen an attempt to load Prince, but his family described the last attempt to load him as being horrific, as well as taking a long time. They were really anxious not to have a repeat performance!

My plan was to help Prince have good associations with the trailer, and I decided to put aside about twenty minutes every day for a week to work towards the end goal.

The idea was to just let Prince walk around the trailer, exploring it on the first day, then just putting his front feet on the ramp the second day, all his feet the next day, fully in by the fourth day, until by the seventh day it was hoped he would be perfectly happy to stand in the trailer with everything closed up around him. At all stages, there would just be lots of repetition, praise and rewards, and most importantly, no force. If we made it into a bit of a game, then Prince may start to enjoy himself.

The whole experience revealed just how much trust Prince had in me. On the second day, when I just asked for him to step on the ramp, he actually offered to go the whole way in. But this would have been too much too soon, and he may have frightened himself. It was important that we proceeded slowly.

Slowly always wins the race in my opinion, and by the end of the week, I was delighted at how well the whole thing had gone. At no point had Prince resisted, and he was relaxed and willing throughout the whole of the training. When I totted up the time spent on this work, I reckon that I had probably only spent the equivalent of an hour. An hour well spent without a doubt.

A week later when Prince went off to his new yard, he loaded like a pro, just walking calmly straight on. I was so proud of him!

The benefits of the training stayed with him. No attempts to load him were made for about six months, but when he was transported to another yard, again he just walked straight on.

Creating good energy and positive associations can make a huge difference, and the horse will not forget.

Saying goodbye

Eventually the time came to say goodbye to Prince.

Although his owners loved him dearly, Becky had moved in with her boyfriend and was living some distance away.

They no longer had the time to devote to Prince, resulting in the heart-breaking decision to sell him.

As devoted owners, they did everything in their power to ensure he went to the best home possible. He spent some time at the yard of a local showjumper and she really progressed his jumping ability, so much so, that it was an effortless process to find him a suitable home.

He was sent on his way with a bag of goodies, including the typescripts of the Animal Communication's and Reiki healings I carried out on him.

I often think about Prince and hope that he is well, happy and loved. I am indebted to him for the connection he forged with me, and the trust he placed in me. He was a horse who touched my heart, and I will always remember him with great fondness.

A self-reflection exercise

- Give yourself time to reflect, making sure there are no distractions and you won't be disturbed.

- Start to connect to your breath, taking deep breaths in through the nose, and out through the mouth.

- When you are fully relaxed, think about one of your animals who may be behaving badly in some way.

Or maybe they have what you may consider a naughty trait to their personality.

- Take the first thing that comes up for you.

- Think deeply about the situation that has come up. Try standing back from it and looking at it from an outsider point of view. Reframe the way you think about it, and consider it from the animal's perspective. Perhaps try and put yourself in the animal's paws/hooves. Are they doing it to get your attention? Could it be a pain or a fear response? Could they be reacting to your energy? Could they be carrying a wound from the past?

- As you think about their behaviour, let go of your anger and frustration, and just let those emotions fade away. Then visualise your animal behaving in a way you would like to see. Engage with your senses – what you are seeing, hearing, smelling and feeling. Allow yourself to feel really good about how well your animal is behaving, and allow the love for your animal to really build up in your heart. Tell them you love them for who they are.

- As these positive emotions take over, think about the changes you need to make to allow your animal to be the best they can be. Ask yourself what needs to be done to bring about the changes you so desire.

See what comes into your mind, then make those changes.

Huge changes can come about in our animals because of the adjustments in our energy and our feelings towards them. Animals are way more intuitive than us, and they can read our feelings very easily. They know exactly how we feel about them, so it is so important to express love and gratitude to them for being in our lives. When we focus on the good things they bring to us rather than the bad, there can be a huge shift in the relationship and in their behaviour.

IVOR

A lesson in boundary setting

"Oh yes I'm the great pretender
Just laughing and gay like a clown
I seem to be what I'm not you see
I'm wearing my heart like a crown."
(Queen)

Identity is as important to animals as it is to us. We all like to be seen for who we truly are. Maybe it is for this reason that whenever I meet an animal for the first time, I greet them with the word, *"Namaste."* This is a traditional Hindu greeting which translates as *"The soul in me sees the soul in you."* To me it is a truly beautiful word, and I always feel that the animals love being greeted in this way. It is like they truly understand, and on an energetic level, I do not doubt it.

I first met Ivor in January 2018. This strong minded, sensitive donkey was going to impress on me how much his identity mattered to him, and he was also going to teach me some important lessons in boundary setting.

His lovely Guardian, Sandy, had invited me to communicate with Ivor and her other donkey Bilbo. I was to follow this up by meeting them in person, the intention being to share some Reiki healing with them.

Both donkeys had been adopted together. They were doing well, and Sandy who had always owned horses before, was doing her utmost to learn everything about donkeys, and to provide them with the very best care she could. Nobody could have devoted more time and effort to these donkeys. To say they had landed on their hooves was an understatement!

Communication

The distance Animal Communication went well, and I felt that I really picked up a lot from the personality and character of each donkey. The two donkeys were like chalk and cheese.

Bilbo, the brown donkey, came across as very warm and friendly, whereas Ivor, the grey donkey, was very different. He warned me that whereas Bilbo would be all over me when I went to visit, he Ivor would be a lot more discerning.

Ivor was without doubt, the more challenging of the two donkeys. But he also made me smile, particularly when he described being born in the wrong body. He stated emphatically that he was way too intelligent for a donkey, and his wisdom was very much wasted, contained as it was in what he considered a most inappropriate body.

Sometimes when I am communicating with animals, I hear the words of a song start playing in my head, and when I read the lyrics, it often supports what the animal has been saying. So when I heard words from Queens' *"The Great Pretender"* it made me smile. Like the words of the song, Ivor just can't reconcile his comical donkey body (his opinion not mine) with the intelligence and wisdom of his mind. And as for donkey sounds, he was so ashamed of the way he sounded that he rarely used his voice. Even though I pointed out how much I love donkeys, and how they had the honour of carrying one of the greatest men who ever lived (Jesus), there was no altering Ivor's opinion of himself.

It also seemed that Ivor was a donkey who very much liked things on his terms. *"And what I can't tolerate"* he emphasized, *"Is people who force things on me and don't respect my boundaries."* I was so looking forward to meeting Ivor. He seemed quite the character!

The meeting

The first meeting with Ivor and Bilbo went very much as Ivor predicted. Bilbo was all over me, and Ivor was keeping a good distance between himself and me. I did follow him into his stable at one point, and he was not at all impressed by my "disrespectful" behaviour. *"How would you like someone to just enter your house before being asked?"* I could hear him grumble. Rather than eat his hay at the front of the stable, he chose to retreat to the back of the stable the moment I entered, glaring at me with his beautiful big donkey eyes. I didn't want to intimidate him, so I retreated out of his stable.

It was a freezing January day, and I knew my tolerance to the cold would last no longer than an hour. As the minutes ticked away, and I became more desperate to form some connection with Ivor, it seemed like I was chasing him around the yard. In my defence, it was one of my earliest attempts at giving Reiki face to face with someone else's animal, but even so, my actions were a mark of desperation. Was it any wonder that Ivor was giving me a wide berth?

Finally, the penny dropped, and I realised that I was doing exactly what Ivor had warned me about in the communication. I was forcing myself on him and not respecting his boundaries at all. How could I have been so stupid?

I let the desperation leave my body and I forced myself to disengage with my ego. I stood still, and concentrated on radiating some positive, loving energy towards Ivor. As I did so, I spoke softly to him and said *"Ivor, I really respect your intelligence. I am so sorry for chasing you around like this. You are clearly a very clever and discerning donkey, and I respect you greatly for that."*

The moment the words left my lips, I noticed a change in Ivor's demeanour. His eyes softened and he started to walk towards me. I kept still and held my arm out towards him. What followed was a really beautiful connection. I started stroking him under his chin and he responded really well to it. Everything was fine between us! I had made a friend!

Sadly though, our time was up. But I did promise Sandy that I would send Ivor some distance healing Reiki and we would see how he responded to it.

Reiki Healing

The main thing to come out of the Reiki session was an awareness of how blocked Ivor's root chakra appeared. In checking out Ivor's chakras (energy centres) I noticed how spiky the energy appeared to be in his root chakra. This very much suggested that his root chakra was blocked and needed clearing.

The root chakra is very much related to feelings of safety and security. When out of balance, the person/animal may demonstrate an inability to feel safe in the world, with everything looking like a potential risk. A blocked root chakra can translate behaviours into those ruled by fear. Having seen Ivor's reaction towards me, and witnessing his distrust and concern, it did not surprise me in the least that Ivor had a blocked root chakra.

I spent most of the session trying to release the block in the root chakra, and by the end of the session it did start to feel better. After another session, it improved yet again.

When I recounted this back to Sandy, she confirmed that something quite amazing had happened to Ivor. The very day after the Reiki healing, she noticed that the kink which he had in his tail had literally dropped out, and he was much more relaxed about her picking up his tail. All the tension just seemed to have vanished. Ivor had carried this kink in his tail from the time he had been with Sandy, but the release of the kink has been a permanent feature. Four years on, it has not returned.

After the Reiki healing, Sandy reported Ivor being a lot more relaxed and accepting. For starters, he no longer retreated to the back of the stable when she entered it. Sandy also felt that now she understood so much more about him, she felt more relaxed around him and this had deepened their connection.

The big surprise for me came when I went to visit Ivor and Bilbo again, a couple of weeks after the Reiki. I was just gob smacked by the changes in Ivor, and could hardly recognise him as the same donkey. Unlike last time, he happily came over to say hello, and when he walked into the stable with me hot on his heels, he cared not a jot. As he stood eating hay at the front of his stable, I stroked his rump. There were no words of admonishment! Just acceptance!

Aversion to grooming

In May 2020, Sandy contacted me again, and asked if I would have another word with Ivor, addressing some of his behaviours. Sandy was concerned that he could be difficult to groom, and she couldn't understand why Ivor would sometimes be ok about wearing his fly mask, yet other days he could be very averse to it, refusing to let her put it on.

Once again, Ivor was going to make me smile with some of his answers, and he was also going to reveal how there can be a big chasm in perception. For instance, Sandy has always expressed to me how much she loves grooming and messing with her boys, but for Ivor this is not an enjoyable pastime, and it is completely disrespectful in his opinion that someone invade his body space and inflict a brush on him. How dare they!

"How would you like it if someone came up to you and just started to give you a body scrub without you asking for it? I guess you wouldn't be too happy? My body, my decision" he huffed at me. Then he went on to deride the whole idea of being clean. He proceeded to point out the huge benefits of being covered in mud, such as protection from the weather, protection from fly bites, and neurological benefits derived from the process of rolling and the energetic properties of the soil. *"Can I help it if you humans don't appreciate how beneficial mud can be?"* he finished curtly.

Then there was the issue of the fly mask. I was just about to be on the receiving end of Ivor's derision again. *"Well, don't I have the option to choose?"* he asks indignantly. *"One day I might decide the flies are irritating me enough to wear it, and another day I may decide that I would rather not have it on. I don't really like them. They make it harder to see, and they can make parts of my face feel hot. You humans just love putting things on us, when we generally prefer to be naked. I prefer covering my face in mud. Please just accept if I don't want to wear it. My decision, my choice, and I will live with the consequences."*

Yep, however much Reiki healing I could send Ivor, there are some things we are never going to change. His strong, independent, sometimes aloof character is part of who he is, and I know Sandy loves him very much for this. It may drive her a bit crazy at times, but the truth is, she wouldn't change him for the world. Ivor keeps her on her toes, and in working out how to deal with his sensitive nature, she has learned an awful lot about caring for and keeping donkeys. He has been a great teacher for her.

Vet visit

Sandy contacted me in November 2020, wondering if I could send Ivor some Reiki healing.

He had received his flu and tetanus vaccination from the vet, and although she was very kind and considerate, and although everything seemed to go fine, the next day Ivor wanted nothing to do with Sandy at all. He wouldn't even let her catch him in the stable, A few days later, Ivor had still not come around. Sandy described that she only had to touch him and he would react with such abruptness that it was like he had been stabbed.

Tuning into him, I felt some discomfort around the base of my neck– it felt stiff and sore. This may be where the injection went in. The message that Ivor seemed to be conveying was that he was suffering a little with some after effects of the injection, and Ivor being Ivor, it had turned him into a bit of a grumpy man who just wanted his own space. He doesn't cope well with discomfort; at these times he really wants his boundaries respected, and he just wants to be left alone, to lick his wounds in private. No different to some people, I guess!

I reassured Sandy of this, advising her that she shouldn't take it personally, and I sent Ivor some Reiki healing. Thankfully, he came around very quickly after that.

Ivor was due another vaccination a couple of months later, so I sent him Reiki the night before. Thankfully, this time there were no ill effects at all. In fact, Sandy was amazed at how good he was – not just with having the vaccination, but the next day she described him as an angel – very quiet and gentle on his walk, and behaving like a "lovely" donkey. She wondered what on Earth I had said or done to him!

I think with all animals, we have to consider which behaviours are down to their character/personality, and which are down to blocked energy fields, unhealed emotional wounds or physical/emotional issues. A distinction does need to be drawn between them. If how they are acting is part of their character, then Animal Communication and Reiki are only going to be partly helpful. Sometimes it is just a case of accepting the animal for who they are. But this can be a huge game-changer, because let's face it, don't we all love being accepted and appreciated for who we are? This can often really deepen the human/animal bond.

Sandy has been a model owner for Ivor, because although there are things she may like to change i.e. his willingness to let her groom and mess with him, she has embraced Ivor wholly for the soul he is. Personally, I also feel that the challenges he has presented her with have actually endeared him to her even more than if he had been a straightforward donkey. Sandy has made no secret of the fact that Ivor really does hold a very special place in her heart. He makes her laugh, and let's face it we all need someone around us who has the ability to put a smile on our face.

Like a lot of animals, Ivor has stretched Sandy in ways she may never have envisaged. She has worked extremely hard to understand the nature of donkeys, recognising how different they are to horses – both in their character and needs, and she has embraced Animal Communication and Reiki healing, even though she had no knowledge of these practices before.

And me! Well I have a soft spot for Ivor too. His communications always make me smile, and he taught me a very valuable lesson in boundary setting, and an even more valuable lesson in following the advice an animal gives in their communication. Ignore what they say at your peril!

He also helped me massively with my confidence. The donkeys I met were exactly how I perceived them to be after the Animal Communication, and then it was so reassuring to actually see for myself the changes in Ivor after the first Reiki healing. Up until then, if people praised my work, I found it hard to believe them and just thought they were being kind. But seeing the changes for myself was an enormous confidence boost.

In the first Animal Communication I carried out with Ivor, he happened to mention that once he made a friend, they were a friend for life, so I guess it was no coincidence that the few times I have walked past his field, he has always come over to say hello, enjoying a good scratch under his chin. I am grateful for his lessons. Who would have thought a donkey could possess such wisdom! At least Ivor should be reassured that his talents haven't been wasted.

A self-reflection exercise

- Give yourself time to reflect, making sure there are no distractions and you won't be disturbed.

- Start to connect to your breath, taking deep breaths in through the nose, and out through the mouth.

- Give some thought to a behaviour in your animal which you would like to change. Reflect on it and consider whether the behaviour is a result of their personality and character, or whether it may be due to blocked energy, or an unhealed wound or physical problem. Could it be a little bit of all of them? If you are unsure, try asking the question out loud, and see what impressions come to mind. If you are still unsure, you could consider asking an Animal Communicator. You may also want to consider whether you are attributing to the behaviour, as very often we can be creating unwanted problems for our animals.

- When you have decided where the behaviour originates from, consider how you can deal with it. If it is just part of their personality, you may need to consider your perception of it, and how you could react to it more positively. How can you express to your animal that you love them for who they are? If it is a physical problem, then you may need to consult a vet. A Reiki or energy healer would be able to help you with blocked energy or an unhealed emotional wound. If you are the problem, then you may want to consider what changes need to be made. Do you need to do any inner work on yourself? There are many horse trainers around now who encourage the riders/handlers to do inner work on themselves, and this often resolves any problems they may be experiencing.

Finally, remember that we all yearn to be loved for who we are. Donkeys are no exception!

ROSIE

A Lesson in Taming the Ego

When man can tame his competitive spirit
Putting aside his need to train and conquer
He will discover that a deep connection
Based on love, respect and empathy
Is far more satisfying
Than a trophy which decorates the room.
The one collects dust
The other celebrates union.

It was a year that will go down in history as one of the most challenging in recent times; all because of a virus that had swept through the world. Everyone had been affected by Covid 19; both physically and mentally. It had cast long shadows over everyone's lives, and we were all feeling worn down by the daily news reports, not to mention the agony and worry of seeing our loved ones succumb to the disease. On top of all that, we had lockdown to cope with as well.

I was one of the lucky ones and feel that I didn't fare nearly as badly as my fellow man. Working part-time at home was not a problem, and having a horse on a DIY yard meant that I was still able to continue with my daily visits to see to her needs. Riding was possible too. So compared to most people, I remained pretty well unscathed.

Nevertheless, it did seem to cause some sort of restlessness in my spirit. I was starting to feel like I needed some sort of change in my life, and this was being channelled into my desire for another animal in our lives. Being guardian to only one animal (my horse Jazz) was just not enough.

As my husband wouldn't even entertain the idea of a dog or cat, then my thoughts started to veer towards taking on another horse. Lauren had been sharing my horse Jazz for a few years, but now that Jazz had fractured her splint bone, competitive riding was off the agenda. Lauren was no different to how I had been at her age – she just loved competing, and with her spending so much time at home due to covid (she was in her 4th year doing a veterinary degree) then it seemed like the right time to buy.

Unsurprisingly, Lauren was absolutely delighted with the idea.

The search for a horse

My methods for finding a horse were a bit different to say the least, as I decided to ask Tiffany, my horse in spirit, if she could find the perfect horse for us. Let's just say that I have very much learned to think outside the box while walking this spiritual path. Nothing is off limits!

You can read how I went about this in Chapter 13, which is all about Tiffany and how she is helping us on the other side.

Within two hours of making my request, Rosie appeared on our radar. In actual fact, although I had been absolutely determined that we would not buy the first horse we saw, and I wanted Lauren to see lots of horses before we made a decision, Rosie was not only the first horse we saw, but the only horse we saw. Talk about meant to be!

The moment I walked in Rosie's stable, I was absolutely won over by her energy, which felt so gentle and healing. It was like being wrapped in a warm, cosy blanket. Lauren felt the same way about her too.

Rosie's advert had described her as being 16.1hh. When I had been perusing adverts, I refused to look at any advert where the horse was over 16hh. With Lauren and I being relatively small, that height felt plenty big enough for me. But it had been Lauren who had come across Rosie's advert and she had persuaded me that one inch should not make a great deal of difference. Well, okay, I could concede to that.

I clearly had a bit of a fixation with height, because the first thing I did when I saw Rosie is compare her to Jazz who is 16hh. *"Yes"* I thought to myself, *"She is about the same height as Jazz."*

Anyway, to cut a long story short, two weeks later, Rosie arrived at our yard. The first thing I thought to myself as she walked off the box was *"Oh my God! She is enormous! How could I possibly have thought she was the same height as Jazz?"*

Measuring tape found, we discovered she was 16.3hh. Strangely, even though both Lauren and I had seen and tried her twice, neither of us had thought she was bigger than advertised. How could we possibly have not noticed? She appeared huge next to Jazz. It was almost like we had to see her as smaller than she was, otherwise I would have been put off by her size.

Life with Rosie

It quickly became apparent that Rosie was a gem of a horse. She was a bit crooked and one-sided in her school work, and her agility and suppleness needed working on; but we prefer horses which need bringing on, as it is satisfying to see the changes. Apart from this, we were blown away by her beautiful, trusting nature, and her ability to try her hardest at whatever we asked her to do.

When we checked her parentage from her passport, we were amazed to discover how well-bred she was. Her father was a hugely successful eventer, and we discovered that her full brother who was born a year after her, had just come sixth in the world eventing championships for seven year olds. This made me wonder how on earth a horse of this breeding quality, possessing such a beautiful temperament, had even been remotely within my budget. Tiffany had pulled off an amazing stunt to bring this stunningly beautiful horse into our family.

Rosie was a wonderful horse for sure, but even lovely horses have their quirks, and there are often challenges at the beginning. Rosie was no exception.

In the beginning, Rosie seemed to lose a lot of confidence. She had been kept in a town environment, where riding had been along busy, main roads, and suburbs. But our yard was slap, bang in the middle of countryside, surrounded by fields, and worse than that, the moment you rode out of the yard, there was a big field full of sheep running alongside the lane you had to walk down. Poor Rosie was absolutely terrified of the sheep, and it seemed very clear that she had never encountered such animals before, as she had no idea what to make of them. *"What on Earth are they?"* she snorted, with her eyes out on stalks.

When we tried Rosie out, we had taken her out on a ride on her own, as well as riding her out on another day with two other horses, where she took it in turns to go in front and behind. On all these occasions, she had behaved impeccably. Yet now, she was only happy to ride out with a person or horse walking out in front of her, as it was all way too scary.

This demonstrates how difficult it can be for horses to adjust to a new home. Not only do they have to deal with moving away from their friends and familiar handlers, but often, they have to adjust to a completely different environment; all which involve different sights, sounds, smells and energies. It is a sensory overload! No wonder that many horses can seem very different to the horse that was tried out.

Thankfully, my Animal Communication skills came to our rescue, and I was able to tune into Rosie to evaluate exactly what her concerns were. It was just a matter of giving her plenty of time to adjust to all the changes and to allow her confidence to develop, which thankfully it did. She now rides out happily on her own, as well as giving other horses a lead.

As I write this, Rosie has been with us for just over a year. She truly is the perfect horse for us and we are all having so much fun together – hacking, attending clinics and competing. We recently bought a little horsebox (I have waited forty years for this) and I can't wait for the warmer weather when we can take Rosie out on some picnic rides.

It is not only us who are benefiting from having this lovely horse in our lives; Jazz is too, for they have formed the most beautiful friendship. They are so attentive and caring towards each other, and even though they are the only two in the field, there is no problem at all if you take one out of the field. Neither of them registers even the slightest concern! It is just heart-warming to witness.

Soul connection message

One night, not long after Rosie had been with us, I had been doing some spiritual work, when I happened to turn on my computer and stare a while at one of Rosie's beautiful pictures on my computer. I had not intended to connect with her, but the following message just flowed straight through:

"My birth was no accident. It was carefully engineered. Planned to the finest detail. So many hopes, dreams and ambitions paved the way for my entrance into the world.

I was bred for power. So man can enjoy the feeling of flying boldly over a fence.

I was bred for movement. So man can experience floating above the ground.

I was bred for ability. So man can succeed.

I was bred for potential. So man can experience triumph and awards.

I was bred for one purpose only; to satisfy man's ego.

People have referred to me as a machine. A powerhouse! How would you feel about being so described?

How would you feel if you were only acknowledged for your physical attributes?

How would you feel if your only value was measured by how fast you could run, or how high you could jump?

I am no different to you. Look deep into my eyes and you can see my soul; feel my desires; witness my dreams; experience the essence of my being.

I am a sentient soul. Just like you, I yearn to be fully witnessed and acknowledged. Not as a machine, but as an intelligent, feeling Being.

When you see me for who I truly am, then you can appreciate my greater gifts; gifts that take you beyond the physical. Look deeper than the surface and you will unearth my real treasures.

Turn away from how I can serve. See me not as a vessel to inflate your ego. Instead, let my essence pour over you, until you are soothed with calm and peace. Allow the serenity of my soul to infuse with yours, until you understand the true meaning of togetherness.

Man thinks he knows it all. He thinks he has all the answers. He creates to appease his ego. But if he looked deeper into his creation, he would unearth the real treasure.

I am not here to serve the ego.

I am here to serve the soul."

Wow! I was just blown away with this. She is speaking on behalf of so many horses. At this moment in time, we are still fixated on what the horse can do for us, and what they can deliver. Few people put the soul of the horse before their athleticism or ability to perform.

But when you feel into the character and personality of the horse, you recognise how individual they are, and how they have important lessons to teach.

Although Lauren does compete Rosie, it is less from an ego perspective and more for the sheer enjoyment of meeting fences right, sailing over them, and then enjoying the feel of speed in the jump-off. And there is no denying that Rosie enjoys herself too. They compete fairly low level, and Lauren is less concerned about the placings, and more interested in the connection and fluidity of their partnership.

No doubt Rosie will have many lessons for Lauren in the future.

"Thank you Rosie for being in our life, blessing us with your beautiful spirit. We do see you for who you are, and we pray that we are worthy of your special soul."

A self-reflection exercise

- Give yourself time to reflect, making sure there are no distractions and you won't be disturbed.

- Start to connect to your breath, taking deep breaths in through the nose, and out through the mouth.

- When you are fully relaxed, think about one of your animals, and consider your relationship with them. Think about what expectations you have of them, or how you expect them to behave. Is your ego getting in the way at all? Are you expecting them to win prizes for you? Try and see yourself from their perspective. Is your relationship equally balanced, or is it one-sided, where you are expecting a lot from them?

- Consider how you could improve things to make the partnership more evenly balanced. What changes might you need to make? If you do expect a lot from them, how could you make changes so that they equally receive a lot from you?

I consider our relationship with the horse very much like a marriage. There needs to be a lot of give and take, yet at this moment in time I do think that the balance is very askew. We expect and often demand so much from our horses, but we are not so willing to give back. Is it any wonder that a horse who is only taken out of the field to be ridden, or for blacksmith/dentist/vet visits, will be more reluctant to be caught or resistant to being taken out of the field? After all, what is in it for him?

So consider how you can give something back and how you can reward your horse. At the moment of typing this, we are enjoying a very wet summer, but the warmth and sunshine is really making the grass grow. Except in our field that is, where I am actually having to put haylage out for Rosie and Jazz. So whenever, we ride Rosie or take her to shows and clinics, we always make sure that after the ride, she spends a minimum of thirty minutes eating some lush grass. This is her reward, and helps her to feel that we are giving something back. It keeps her happy and fulfilled, as she recognises this is a fair exchange.

Whenever we put in the effort to reward our animals, it is inevitable that these generous hearted souls will notice and naturally want to reciprocate. This is how a more equal partnership develops!

THE HORSE'S TRUTH

No accidental birth for me
Everything planned meticulously
A stallion found to further the odds
Producing offspring to impress the Gods.

Bred for speed; built for power
All to make competitors cower
I had no say in my soul's life plan
Designed to appease the ego of man.

Look into my eyes, what do you see?
I am much more than a prodigy
Like you, I too possess a soul,
A longing to be seen as complete and whole.

Man creates for wealth and gain
Satisfying his greed and urge for fame
By casting his ego to one side
Much greater treasures he would find.

Nothing in life is as it seems
Dive deep to find what really gleams
It isn't the shiny or the bright
But rather what is out of sight!

As our souls merge then we will find
A love so great, our hearts will bind
Together, forever, across time and space
Now we are in our heavenly place!

FIONA SUTTON

PART 4 – ANIMALS IN SPIRIT

True love is forever.
Physical separation cannot break the bonds of a soul connection.
When we lay our animals to rest
We can do so knowing that part of their soul remains with us
There is no separation.

The death of a much loved animal is torturous to us animal lovers, and is made worse by the fact most animals don't live very long lives. In comparison to our own lives, they are very short, meaning that in our own lifespan, we can be welcoming in many animals. Sadly, this also means that we have to say goodbye to as many too. It is the real downside to being an animal lover!

In this section of the book, I want to demonstrate that when our animals leave the physical plane, it needn't be the end of our relationship with them. On the contrary, although we can't see them or sense them, I have absolutely no doubt that the moment we think about them, they are instantly drawn to our side. I also believe that they can help us on the other side in ways that we may never have thought possible. Certainly this has been my experience, and I hope after reading the following stories, you will consider it a possibility.

The bonds we share with some of our animals can be so strong that I have come to believe that it isn't just people we share a soul relationship with; on the contrary, it can be with animals too. My thinking has now evolved around the idea that we can have a soul contract with an animal(s) before coming into this physical incarnation. Through this contract, we make agreements whereby we propose to each help and support the other through the physical journey. This help also consists of lessons and teachings, the idea behind it being to help each other to evolve. But even when one transitions to the other side, the bond is never severed, and contact can still be strong. Yes, it has changed in nature, but it is still there.

Each of the three stories in the following chapters, demonstrate what is possible.

In the story of Candy, my dog, I am revealing an amazing truth – you don't have to be a gifted medium to connect with those on the other side. In truth, it is actually very simplistic and easy. So easy in fact, that we have all just been blind to what is right under our noses. This chapter I promise you will be a revelation!

The chapter on Tiffany will reveal how much our loved ones can help us on the other side. Sometimes we have to ask, other times they can just put ideas into our heads, guiding us to be our most creative. It does make me wonder sometimes, how many of our thoughts come from our spirit team? Yes, those animals with whom we share a soul contract, being part of our soul family, are definitely part of our spirit team.

Finally, I have included a chapter on my friend's dog Tess, to demonstrate how it is possible to receive messages from the other side and to pick them up using our physical senses.

Be prepared to have your eyes well and truly opened!

CANDY

Signs Delivered From the Other Side

Connecting through a loving heart
Is the bridge between the worlds
Allowing a letter to be sent every day,
Sealed with a kiss.

In some ways I feel that I was a complete throw-back in my family. As far as I know, in a huge line-up of ancestors, I was the first one to be born who was completely crazy about animals. My sister, who was born two years later, was a close second. Goodness knows where we inherited it from, because it was something that was completely new on both sides of our ancestral field.

From the moment we could talk, both my sister and I were begging for a pet. My parents were so far removed from the nature of animals that they didn't even recognise them as sentient beings. Years later, my dad would thank us for opening his eyes to the wonder of animals.

To satisfy our animal cravings, we were bought a couple of tortoises when I was four years old. But of course it didn't stop there! Owning a dog and/or horse was my number one aim.

When I was seven, my dad developed a bad bout of flu. Cruelly, my sister and I relentlessly badgered my dad for a dog, recognising that while his defences were down we had the best chance of him agreeing to our wishes. Who won't give anything for a bit of peace and quiet when they are ill? My dad was no exception. So he eventually gave in to our demands, and agreed that we could have a dog. Being a man of his word, he kept his promise, resulting in Candy, a stunningly beautiful apricot poodle, joining our family.

Candy was everything we could have dreamed of in a dog and more. She was so clever, intelligent and fun to be around. We all just adored her, and she us. It was a match made in Heaven!

Needless to say, her death when she was 13 years old left each of us devastated. My parents swore they couldn't go through this again, and so that was the end of dog owning for our family.

I grieved terribly for Candy. Never before had I cried so many tears for anything. After weeks of crying, I just reached the point where there were no more tears left. My heart was just broken!

Dreams

It is hard to say when the dreams of Candy started. It was possibly some years after she had transitioned. The dreams were welcomed and brought so much comfort. They were always vivid and seemed so real. From what I understand now, I believe them to be dream visitations.

Dream visitations differ from normal dreams in that they are acutely vivid; you remember them clearly when you wake up, and indeed many years later. Also, the sequence and the events in the dream seem very much like real life. When you get dreams like this, I do believe that it is your loved one in spirit form meeting up and spending time with you on the ethereal plane.

These dreams of Candy were always very similar. I would be absolutely overjoyed at seeing her again, and I would always say, *"So you didn't really die after all. That was just a dream."*

And this is the message I believe Candy was trying to pass on: she hadn't died! She may have dispensed with her body, but her soul was very much still alive, having just moved into another dimension. Once I followed the spiritual path, fully understanding this concept, the dreams stopped. She didn't have to prove this to me anymore.

More recently, I had a wonderful dream. We were at the seaside and Candy was running in and out the sea with me, in total joyful abandonment. We were both having so much fun! But the strange thing here was that Candy never liked the sea. She would come down to the sea with us because she didn't want to be left out, but it would be most begrudgingly, with her tail under her legs. Her dislike of water probably originated from her falling in a lake when she was a puppy. Although she swam to the side and we were able to snatch her out of the water, it did leave her with a lifelong fear of water of any sorts. Yet here she was in this dream having the best fun ever. It felt like she was saying *"Look at me now. I am a changed dog and have overcome my fear!"*

Meeting through meditation

It doesn't matter how long ago your animal transitioned, the bonds of love never weaken, and the potential is always there to meet them on the ethereal plane, in dreams or in meditation.

It is said that in order to meet with our loved ones in spirit we have to raise our vibration, and they have to lower theirs. When you pass over, you become a light body which vibrates at a much higher rate than when you are in the denser energies of physical form. It is reckoned that this is why we can't see those in spirit, because their faster vibration makes them invisible to us.

Love is one of the highest vibrations, so 37 years on from Candy's transition, I decided to connect to her through our bond of love.

I was lying on a beach in Corfu. Bored with reading and with nothing better to do, the idea came into my mind to try and connect to Candy. I had connected to animals in spirit through my Animal Communication, and I always enjoyed the wisdom they imparted, so it seemed a great idea to talk to Candy. How was she doing? What was she doing? Would I be able to bring her to me just by thinking about her?

So the intention to connect with Candy was very strong indeed. Firstly, I slowed down my brain waves through deep breathing, inducing the light trance state of the alpha brain state which is needed when doing this work.

Then I allowed my mind to wander, resurrecting all the wonderful memories of Candy. The first day we picked her up and brought her home is imprinted on my mind. Even though I was so young at that time, the memory of her excitement at being the "chosen one" and her happily curling up on my lap is still so very clear and feels like yesterday.

It was so easy to connect to the love we shared and the fun times we had experienced together. Candy had lived for her walks, and she particularly loved running loose over a nearby beauty spot. It was different in those days, and you didn't have to monitor your dog so closely. Just as well really, because Candy was in my dad's words, *"Like a greyhound in disguise."* She had so much energy, which would be released in continuous running backwards and forwards. At times, she would appear as just a dot in the distance, but she would always come running back. Sometimes we would hide from her, but of course, with her excellent nose, it only took her seconds to sniff out our hiding place.

My sister and I felt incredibly reassured by her presence. As quite fearful kids, feeling uneasy in the dark, we always felt totally safe and protected when Candy was around. She would have protected us with her life. Although she wasn't supposed to lie on our beds at night, we circumvented this rule quite successfully. Candy would come upstairs with us and lie on our beds. The moment she heard my dad coming up the stairs she would dive under the bed, refusing to come out until he left the room. We would sleep peacefully those nights with our protector by our sides.

Some of the memories made me chuckle. Candy was so intelligent and she could work out the meaning of words quite easily, so we would always have to change them. If someone brought up the word *"walk"* she would bark excitedly and run to the drawer which housed her lead. So we would start spelling it out instead, but then she would work that out, and you had to change it to something else.

Due to her high intelligence, she was incredibly clued up. If you were holding treats she would be the most obedient dog ever. You could ask anything of her – sit, lie, wait, shake a paw, jump over jumps etc. You name it, she would do it. But if you didn't hold a treat, she would look at you bemusedly with a *"You must be kidding"* look on her face, and would completely ignore you. Those memories made me laugh.

Some memories weren't so good. Like the time when she was around nine, a dog tried to drag her out of the garden by hooking his back legs around hers. We were getting ready to go to school, and some friends had called around to walk with us. Candy's screaming alerted me something was wrong, and running into the garden I was spectacle to the horrible sight of this dog dragging her along the ground.

Thankfully, I was able to frighten him off, but Candy was like a person who had been abused. She was traumatized! She tried to console herself by getting lots of fuss and attention from me and my friends, but the scars stayed with her. Before this, she had loved playing with dogs, but from this moment on, she was very wary and suspicious of other dogs.

Candy had always been a bit of a Houdini. Despite dad doing everything he could to contain her, and although we had a fairly large garden, Candy would regularly discover the weak spot in the fencing and would take herself into the fields at the back of the house. Such was her desire for fun and adventure. On one of these trips out, a very gentle dog from up the road took her under his wing, helping her to regain some of the trust in dogs she had lost.

I tried to put the bad memories to the back of my mind, and just concentrate on the better ones. I needed to keep my vibration high if I was going to stand any chance of connecting with Candy, and so the feelings of love and joy needed to dominate.

Another memory made me laugh. Candy had given us very clear signs that she wanted puppies. She had adopted one of our squeaky toy puppets (remember Sooty and Sweep?) – namely a squeaky Sweep. Well, she would walk everywhere holding him in her mouth and would be constantly cuddling up to him. She even underwent a false pregnancy. On the vet's advice that she should be allowed puppies, we decided to let her spend a day with a friend's poodle. The idea was that we would just leave them together in the garden for the day and let nature take its course. The only problem; Candy loved playing with other dogs, but she had no interest in romantic liaisons. I still remember going around to pick her up. Everyone was in fits of laughter! Candy had given this dog the run around all day. She had got on great with him, happily playing and running around with him, but there was no chance of puppies! She was still happily bouncing around and full of energy, this other dog was just flat out! This was the beginning of the end as far as puppies were concerned.

At other times, Candy really encouraged my sister and I to behave better and more responsibly. Who would have thought a dog could teach you these things? On one memorable occasion, my sister and I had got into an argument over something and started pushing each other around. Candy started screaming and jumped in between us, standing on her rear legs and trying to push us apart. It was so surprising and shocking, that it just stopped my sister and I dead in our tracks. It was so horrifying to realise that we had caused her such anguish, and we both felt utterly ashamed. Never again would we resort to such childish behaviour! Our dog had truly shown us up.

As all the memories came flooding back, it made me feel so incredibly grateful that we had experienced such a wonderful, fun-loving dog in our lives. She really had injected so much laughter, joy and love into our family. I started to recall her smell, and the feel of her soft, silky curls under my fingertips. I know I am biased, but I have never seen such a beautiful poodle ever as Candy. She really was the best!

By allowing myself about thirty minutes to resurrect my memories, I really felt that I was pulling her essence into my energy field, helping to pull her towards me. As I pictured her in my mind's eye standing in front of me, I noted her appearance as a young, vibrant dog, her beauty and energy radiating even more brilliantly.

Then, I started talking to her in my head like I would a person. I knew that she was appearing to me in a form that I recognised, but really now she is a soul, needing no body, she can take on any form she likes.

We enjoyed our conversation together and it felt real. I apologised to her for things that I wished I had done differently, like walking her more when she was younger. Once I got into horses, I was so swept away with riding and hanging out at stables that I did neglect walking Candy. Thankfully, for the last few years of her life, I had started to pay more attention to her needs and wants, and my sister and I between us were making sure that we spent time every day with her, running through the fields. But some part of me wished that I had done this earlier, and I have long felt guilty about putting my own needs and wants before hers.

But in my conversation with her now, it seems that she too wished she had acted differently. She apologised for being jealous and not allowing us to give a home to a stray dog we had found (my friend's family gave her a home instead).

As we both made our apologies to each other, she wisely pointed out that none of us are perfect. We come to Earth to learn lessons, and to help each other to grow and evolve. The main thing, she pointed out, is that we loved each other unconditionally, and that is the greatest gift we can give another. Yes, in hindsight there are always things we could have done differently or better, but those recognitions grow out of our evolving journey. *"What matters is where we are now"* she rightly conjectured.

Candy reassured me that she was close by and with us whenever we thought about her. She tried to pass on the feeling of freedom and limitlessness that she is experiencing on the other side – this was the most amazing feeling and very hard to put into words. It seems she is not planning another Earthly incarnation any time soon, but she will be with me, helping and loving me, when it is my time to pass over. As she was my protector in bodily form, she is still my protector now, helping me in ways that I am completely oblivious.

We must have chatted for about twenty minutes. There were situations that had arisen when she was with me in this Earthly life, which she now allowed me to see through her eyes. She helped me understand that when she buried the bread we had thrown out for the birds, it was because she regarded the garden as her own and no other animal was allowed in. Her duty, she felt, was to protect us and keep everything out of the garden, birds included.

Finally, it was time to say goodbye. My family, lying on the sunbeds around me, were making murmurings about going to get some lunch. The thought suddenly entered my head. Was this meeting with Candy real, or was it all just a story in my head? It seemed important to know. It certainly felt very real, but I needed much more proof than just a feeling. The human side of me wanted some sort of validation that this had been a true soul meeting. It may be unreasonable to ask, but I really wanted proof.

Amazing Signs

I decided to make a request. *"If this is real, and we are really talking to each other, can you please gift me a song?"* I asked her. *"We are going to have lunch at one of the tavernas along the beach, so can you please allow me to hear your song at this time? And just so that I know it is from you, can you please make it an old song from the 1960's, a love song, and one that I will enjoy listening to? Oh, and if there is a message in it, that would be great too."*

What was I thinking? This was asking an awful lot. Despite having received some wondrous signs over the years, even I had to admit that I was really pushing the boat out here. This was a very specific request indeed and inside a very limited timescale. One thing was for sure though. If it did indeed manifest, then it would be fantastic proof that my conversation with Candy had been real.

Having been witness to many signs and synchronicities over the years, I no longer believe in coincidence. They just don't exist in my world anymore. The secret when you ask for signs is to let go of the need to receive them. You make your request and you let it go by putting it out of your mind. A sure fire way of not receiving a sign is to keep looking for it. This act of desperation just lowers your vibration and blocks the sign from appearing.

So, I did let the idea go. So much so in fact, that I didn't even notice that the taverna we were sitting in for lunch wasn't even playing any music. After a light lunch, we were walking back to the beach when we decided to buy ice-creams. As we stood eating them, the clear sounds of music floated our way. I started listening a bit distractedly, but on recognising the song, I started to sing along to it in my head. Yes, this was a love song I had always enjoyed listening to, and it had always touched my heart. The idea of two lovers being separated and sending a letter every day sealed with a kiss had always felt touchingly beautiful to me. It really spoke volumes to my sensitive soul. But wait a minute...could this be my song? Was it written in the 1960's?

I am not a person who is connected to her phone. So it was sometime later that I Googled the song, *"Sealed with a Kiss"* and discovered that it was written in 1960 and became a hit in 1962. I gasped in disbelief! A love song – Yes! A 1960's song – Yes! Did it have a message? Absolutely! My dog was giving me a very clear sign that although she is not with me physically, she is sending me a letter every day from heaven sealed with a kiss. This understanding made me want to cry with joy. This song was just perfect!

I would like to say that this was all the proof needed, to convince me that my conversation with Candy was real. But there is something about having a wonderful holiday and then having to face the reality of going back to work preparing tax returns. It brings you back down to Earth with a solid bump!

So, a few days after my return from holiday, I began to question whether it had all just been an amazing coincidence. It shows my low state of mind, because being a doubting Thomas is not normally something I can be accused of.

Now I was being greedy. *"Ok,"* I said out loud. *"If you really did gift that song for me, then please give me a sign today which will leave me in no doubt whatsoever."*

All it took was two hours. Just two hours!

On visiting my parents, I learned that their shower had stopped working. Whilst sifting through their cabinet, I pulled out the paperwork relating to the shower. A newspaper cutting fell to the floor. As I bent to pick it up, I could barely believe what I was seeing. The first line had been cut through, so left staring me in the face, in big bold lettering was the remainder of the headline *"SEALED WITH A KISS."*

It transpired that on the other side of the cutting was an advert for the shop where dad had bought the shower from, and he had just placed this with the paperwork.

This was truly amazing! I just felt awash with gratitude and happiness. How was it possible to doubt now?

Well, my dear readers, I absolutely hate to admit it, but doubt I did. A week later, as I drove out of Tesco's carpark the thought entered my head, *"Could it all just have been two amazing coincidences?"*

"No!" screamed the Universe, and just to prove a point, there are no prizes for guessing what started playing five minutes later on my Spotify's Daily Mix. Although I had been listening to Daily Mix for months, this song had never played before and I have never listened to it through Spotify, or through any other device. In fact, until our holiday, I hadn't heard it in years.

How could anyone now say that this was just a coincidence? My elation, gratitude and joy knew no bounds. This was such great proof that I had indeed being talking to my much loved dog in spirit, and the messages (including the one contained in the words of the song) had brought me incredible comfort.

It doesn't matter how long ago a loved one has passed, we still miss them and long for contact, and now I had absolute proof that it was easier to connect with a loved one in spirit than I could ever have imagined. It wasn't even necessary to create sacred space, or light a candle. We can just do it. Even lying on a beach surrounded by lots of people! All that is required is intention, focus, love and trust. Yes, it might seem that we are just making it all up in our heads, but this isn't so.

Perhaps we need to change our limiting beliefs here. Unlike a lot of people, I have always had the deepest respect for mediumship. But the long held belief has always been that you have to be born with the gift for it, and people often advertise themselves as descending from a long line of mediums. But what if we all have a gift for it? What if mediumship is as easy as having a conversation in your head with a deceased loved one? We dismiss it because we don't ever presume it can be that easy or straightforward. The assumption is always made that a medium hears voices which aren't their own, or sees things outside their normal vision or mind's eye, but that isn't true for all mediums. More and more mediums themselves are now claiming that we all have the ability to do this work, and many are now preferring to teach it rather than performing readings.

This is not dismissing the work that mediums do. There are some incredible mediums out there, doing amazing work and bringing comfort to many people, and it goes without saying that connecting to others loved ones is much harder than connecting to your own. So that is where gifted mediums really step into their power. But even so, I do think the potential is there for each and every one of us to flex our spiritual muscles and discover our innate, natural ability to connect with our loved ones in spirit. In truth, the same skills are utilised as in Animal Communication, so if you can do the one, you can do the other. I am just passionate about helping people recognise that we all have the ability to do this.

A self-reflection exercise

- Have the intention to connect with one of your animals in spirit. If it helps, hold their photograph in front of you and connect with the essence of their Being.

- Make sure there are no distractions and you won't be disturbed.

- Start to connect to your breath, taking deep breaths in through the nose, and out through the mouth.

- Close your eyes and start to think about your animal and bring your memories alive. Particularly focus on the fun, joy and love you shared. Enable your heart to expand with love and gratitude for having them in your life. This will not only raise your vibration, but it will also help you to connect through the love you hold in your heart. Try to avoid feeling sad because this will just lower your vibration and it will make the connection difficult.

- With your eyes closed, visualise your animal in front of you. Imagine them appearing and feel joy at seeing them again. Take in their physical appearance and trust that you are really talking to them. Don't block yourself by thinking it is all in your imagination. Where does imagination come from after all? Just go along with the idea that it really is this simple. Allow the conversation to flow. Don't question it. Just let it happen naturally.

- When you have finished, ask your animal to give you a sign that they really have been talking to you. It may be that you ask them for something specific, or you may prefer to leave it open. Whatever you ask for, let go of the need to see it happen. Forget you have asked and see what transpires.

- Believe that your meeting was real. Feel immense gratitude and love in your heart that your animal has appeared to you and this is even possible. Miracles do happen! All the time if we are open to them. Western belief, with its emphasis on logical thinking, has closed us off to the magic of what is possible. Recognise this and be thankful that you are open enough to circumvent this brainwashing. Allow yourself to feel the immense love in your heart washing over you, and thank your animal for them blessing you with their presence. We are all richer for these rendezvous.

If only people realised that when an animal passes, it is not the end, but a new beginning. You have the love bond with the animal which grew and developed during your Earthly life together, and it is this bond which now allows you to start over in a new and changed relationship with your animal. One where your animal can share the wisdom of their passing, and where they can help you grow spiritually. Helping you to grow and evolve, doesn't stop with physical separation. On the contrary, having gained their wings, they can help you grow yours!

TIFFANY

Help From the Other Side

*A soul contract doesn't end when one leaves their physical body.
As long as both parties are willing, each can continue to assist the other.*

After receiving the healing from the two horses, as described in the first chapter, there was never any doubt in my mind that my relationship with Tiffany would continue. Yes, it would be different than when we were both in our physical bodies, but I knew that we would be able to meet together in the ethereal plane; a place outside time and space, which is accessible through dreams or meditation.

The events surrounding Tiffany's transition had really cracked my mind wide open. Everything I thought I knew had just slipped away. My mind had experienced a whole new wave of consciousness, leaving me hungry to learn everything I could about spirituality.

In meditation, we can allow ourselves to float outside our third dimensional reality, into a beautiful, peaceful awareness. Through regular meditation, I started to really look forward to leaving my present day cares behind, and accessing a place which was rich in colours, beauty and serenity. The more I practiced, the more I was able to picture, hear, feel and sense this beautiful utopia that existed in my mind. I would start to really look forward to that part of the day when I could just release my thoughts, and enter this beautiful, spiritual world of my imagination. It is amazing how when you focus, everything comes so vividly to life.

Very quickly, I learned how easy it was to meet angels, spirit guides, and transitioned loved ones in this special place. The first time I called Tiffany to me, she appeared in a haze of light, looking radiant, spirited, young and utterly beautiful. It was so wonderful to see how happy and well she looked. I noted that her coat was lighter than I remembered, but when I dug out my photos of her when she first came into my life, her coat was indeed lighter than it had been at the end of her life. I had forgotten these lighter shades of brown, which she had now taken on as a reflection of her younger self.

I often called Tiffany to me in meditation, and she never failed to answer my call. One day, when we were having our usual greeting, she gifted me with a sunflower and she asked me why this was so significant. *"Well,"* I spluttered, *"You gifted me with one when you transitioned, to let me know that you were in a beautiful place."*

"Yes, but why today?" she replied. *"What is significant about today?"*

A thought crossed my mind. No, it couldn't be, surely not! I called out to my daughter who was walking past my bedroom door. *"What is today's date?"* I called out. Her reply left me reeling. It was the first anniversary of the day the sunflower appeared.

I have to confess right here that I am not one to keep a tab on meaningful dates and anniversaries, but I did feel really guilty that I had been completely oblivious that it was exactly a year on from Tiffany's transition and it hadn't even entered even a remote part of my awareness. What could I do but apologise profusely.

Tiffany's reaction was not what I expected. She seemed amused by my discomfort, and more than that, she seemed absolutely delighted. She explained to me that to her this was a really good sign, as it was proof that I was moving forwards with my life, and not dwelling in the past. *"So many people hang on to their sorrow and can't let it go, but that is not what we on the other side want for you,"* she explained. *"It doesn't serve you, and it doesn't serve us either. When you live joyfully, looking ahead in your life, not back, then you are living for us as much as for yourself. That is a life well lived and we too can feel the energising vibration. It helps us on our journey too."* Tiffany always knew how to make me feel better about myself.

In the years since Tiffany's transition, there have been many ways in which I felt Tiffany was guiding me. Like the time when I woke up over Easter, and I just knew that she wanted me to tell the story of her transition in six instalments on a popular Facebook horse group I was a member of. I was astounded by how popular my retelling of her story was, and a few people reached out to me to let me know how inspired and touched they had been by the miracles that had occurred. As well as this, her story was recounted in several popular authors' books, and in one of the big named horse magazines. I would never have had the confidence to take these steps on my own, but with Tiffany by my side, it all seemed an effortless process.

Information from the other side

One particular event really stands out, proving to me that our loved ones in spirit do still want to help us as much as they can. All we have to do is ask. It really is that easy!

It was about five years after Tiffany had transitioned. Lauren (my daughter) and I were on the yard, and she had ridden my horse, Jazz. It was before Lauren had her own car, and we were sharing mine. Lauren had planned to go and visit Silver, her old loan pony who was kept about thirty minutes away, and she was also going to ride him and then have some catch up time with his owner, Vicky. It was agreed that she would take the car and I would walk home, as it was only about a twenty-five minute walk.

Lauren left in my car, and I proceeded to muck out Jazz's stable. Suddenly, a horrible thought struck me. My house keys were on my car keys and I had no way of getting in to my home. Not a problem, I thought, I could just ring Lauren and ask her to get a move on. That was when I discovered another problem. My phone was completely dead – I had done my usual trick of letting the battery run down.

Someone offered to ring Lauren for me, but her number was in my dead phone and I had no idea what it was. Remembering my own number is hard enough, let alone recalling the numbers of my friends and family.

The only thing this lady was able to do, was to leave Lauren a message through Facebook, but I knew there was a good chance she wouldn't see it. Sure enough, an hour later, she hadn't responded to it and had clearly not seen it.

What could I do to kill time? It was actually a really nice, warm, summery day, so I decided to take one of the horse rugs into Jazz's field, which had once been Tiffany's field, lay it on the spot where Tiffany had transitioned and carry out a meditation.

So that is what I did. I sat on the rug, carried out some deep breathing and relaxation exercises, and then I started meditating. At some point, I invited Tiffany into my space, and typically, she appeared instantly, looking radiant and beautiful. After some general chit-chat, I decided to ask her about my predicament. What could she tell me? I asked her whether Lauren would see the Facebook message, and she informed me that she wouldn't see it until she arrived back home. Next, I asked what time she would arrive back home, and her prompt reply quite surprised me. *"She will arrive back at 1.45pm."* Finally, I asked her if she would come and pick me up, and I learned that she would come instantly.

I decided to put complete faith in the information I was hearing. My connection to Tiffany felt strong, made stronger by the fact that I was actually sitting in the exact same spot she had left her Earthly body. Even after all these years, I felt her energetic imprint in this spot.

However, just to edge my bets, I decided not to rush home and then possibly be left sitting on the wall. Instead, I decided to take my time. Do a few more jobs, before walking home.

About ten minutes into my walk home, I passed the field of Ivor and Bilbo, the donkeys I wrote about in an earlier chapter. The gate to their field was set back from the road, so I turned in to say hello to them. They both came over and greeted me warmly. It was so heart-warming to see the change in Ivor. No longer the donkey who wanted nothing to do with me, he was now really enjoying the fuss and attention, and seemed very aware of my previous encounters with him.

Looking at my watch, I noticed that the time was 1.53pm. The thought struck me that if things were to proceed as Tiffany had promised, then Lauren would be coming along the road any minute now. Just then, I heard the sound of a car engine and I just knew it was Lauren. So strong was my knowing, that a slight craziness took me over, and I actually did a jump out of the trees into the road, waving at her to stop. All I can say is that it was such a good job it was her, because any other driver would have thought there was a complete madwoman in the road. The look of shock on Lauren's face was completely priceless and never to be forgotten.

Getting in the car and comparing notes it appeared that the information Tiffany had given me was spot on. Pulling on to the drive at exactly 1.45pm, she had only then noticed the Facebook message, and had immediately set out to pick me up. We were both completely blown away by the accuracy of the details Tiffany had passed on to me, and I felt incredibly grateful and blessed to still be able to communicate with her in such a meaningful way. Wowzers doesn't even get close to how I felt that day!

Finding a horse for Lauren

Lauren was in her fourth year of her veterinary degree, when I decided that the time was right to buy another horse.

Since Silver had gone back home three years earlier, Lauren had been sharing my horse, Jazz, but I had this really strong feeling that Jazz was going to be retired soon. Although she was seventeen and was extremely fit and healthy, this feeling would not leave me. In actual fact, about eight months later, Jazz became very ill with a viral infection, leaving her with Atrial Fibrillation; a condition which enforced her retirement. My intuition had been spot on!

As well as the feeling Jazz was going to be retired, I also knew that Jazz really wanted another horse to share her field with. Although she was on a DIY livery yard with lots of horses around her, they were all kept in individual paddocks, and this is not the same as having another horse to share the field with. For starters, it is impossible to groom each other over a rustic fence with a wire running along the top. Jazz was lonely and had told me. She was desperate to have a friend with whom she could share the delights of mutual grooming. So it was for this reason as much as any, I decided that the time was right to look for another horse.

Lauren was spending a lot of time at home because of covid, so buying another horse would be a great distraction for her, and would help compensate for missing out on university life, and being away from her friends. Needless to say, Lauren was overjoyed with the decision.

My means of finding a horse were very different from most peoples. For a start, I knew that I wanted Tiffany to play a part in our decision making. She had already proven how much help she could give, so handing the responsibility over to her seemed a perfectly rational, sensible decision, although a lot of people might question this.

It was not a good time to be looking for a horse. Covid, with all its lockdown restrictions, had resulted in people working from home and being furloughed. So, with time and money, and desperate to escape the restrictions of lockdown, more and more people were deciding to buy a horse. This, as well as the reduction in breeding, had significantly reduced the pool of horses available to buy, and the price of horses had shot up. Although this was September, when the price of horses normally drops significantly, horses were selling at the highest prices ever.

So, when I set out my list of requirements for the horse that was to come into our lives, it seemed an almost impossible ask. We were looking for a horse that would allow Lauren to do some affiliated jumping, possibly some low-level eventing, but at the same time would be quiet and safe enough for me to ride too. We wanted a horse with a lovely temperament who would get on well with Jazz, and one that would be easy to handle. As for price, I was careful to set a limit. No way was I going to pay silly money for a horse! I also set out a limit on how far we were prepared to travel. The horse had to be within a thirty mile radius. One thing was blatantly obvious: I was asking for hell of a lot!

Lauren was in Bristol at the time, but she was about to come home for two weeks, so we felt this was the ideal time to try out a few horses.

I wrote down the ideal horse we were looking for, and then I carried out a meditation, in which I connected to Tiffany. To make it even more special, a candle was lit, and I surrounded myself with some newly acquired crystals. In fact, this was the first time I had used them. My connection with Tiffany felt strong, and I read out the requirements for the horse we wished to come into our lives. I asked Tiffany if she could help us find such a horse.

Just two hours later, Lauren rang me. She had found a horse she wanted to look at. Despite the fact that I had been insistent about trying out lots of horses, Rosie was the only horse we saw. Her coming into our lives was so meant to be. She has been absolutely perfect for us, fulfilling everything we had desired in a horse. I still can't believe our luck, and I am indebted to Tiffany for finding us such a beautiful, kind and giving horse.

Finding a home for Rosie

The next problem we had was finding a home for Rosie, as the yard we had Jazz on was full and there was quite a waiting list to join.

With no availability anywhere, there was only one thing left to do. Could Tiffany come to our rescue yet again?

I needn't have worried. Just hours after asking Tiffany to help us find a yard for Rosie, a friend messaged to alert me to the fact that a vacancy had materialised at a lovely yard only five minutes away from the yard Jazz was on. In short, the yard was perfect for us, and just a couple of weeks later, Rosie arrived on the yard. This would be the yard that we would eventually move Jazz to, meaning that the two of them are now happily sharing a field together. It has worked out perfectly!

A self-reflection exercise

- Have the intention to connect with one of your animals in spirit and ask for them to come to you in a dream. This can often be the easiest way for your animal to connect, as you are in a much more receptive state when asleep. The term "dream visitation" is used to describe the phenomena of your loved one visiting you in a dream. You know when it is a visitation because you may sense divine love flowing to or from you, and the dream will seem very real and you will remember it clearly on awakening. These experiences really do stand out from normal dreams, and there is no doubting that you have met your loved one on the ethereal plane.

- To prepare yourself for this dream rendezvous, you may want to spend a lot of time in the day thinking about your animal, and recalling all the good memories of your time together. It is good to really focus on the love and fun times you shared. Feeling gratitude for the time you spent together and for having them in your life will also help to raise your vibration, which will make it easier for your animal to reach you.

- While you are lying in bed, try thinking about your animal again. It may be a good idea to look at pictures of them before you go to bed. Set the intention that you wish to meet your animal on the ethereal plane, and if possible, say this out loud. You could set your intention by saying, *"Thank you (name) for meeting me in my dreams, and thank you for allowing me to remember the dream when I awake."*

- As you drift off to sleep, try keeping your focus on them.

- You may have to repeat this exercise for a few days or even weeks before it actually happens. But know that it will. For setting the intention and having belief in the process makes it inevitable, although sometimes it can happen when you release the need for it to happen. If we are trying to force it, then this can be block to them appearing, so it can be a bit of a balancing act.

There is only one thing left to say on completing this chapter: please don't ever doubt that the relationship with a loved one ends on death. It will if you allow it, but conversely the potential is also there for it to grow and evolve. At the end of the day, the choice is yours! Choose wisely.

TESS

A Kiss From the Other Side

Who said that kisses stop when one leaves their body?
Increase your sensitivity and you will discover the truth.
Death does not have to end anything,
Not even a physical relationship.
To think otherwise
Is a great error in your thinking.

About six months after stepping on to my spiritual path, I had a very unusual experience. I had washed my hair (not so unusual!), but as I stepped out of the bathroom I was hit by a very strong, overpowering smell. What it was I had no idea, because my sense of smell has always been pretty well defunct. Those are rare times when I get a whiff of someone's perfume, or the smell of a room I have just walked into. These are not common occurrences for me, and have happened pretty infrequently in my life. So this smell was baffling, and I had no idea what to compare it to.

Over the coming months and years, this ghostly smell would happen quite frequently. It would appear instantly, and it would disappear just as quickly. Nobody else would be able to smell anything, but for me it was overbearing. Sometimes it would last minutes, other times, hours. It was intriguing!

It was only when we had someone come to the yard to try out their aromatherapy oils on the horses, that I was able to associate the smell with something. As I put my nose into one of the bottles to smell it, I instantly recognised it as being "the ghostly smell." It was comforting to know what it finally was, even though I had no idea why this smell was appearing so randomly.

There was only one answer that made any sense. It must be someone in the spirit world trying to grab my attention. I had no idea who, and would never really get to the bottom of it, but in the end I connected it to my Native American spirit guide, Kali, as it appears that Native Americans used aromatherapy oils.

This was my first initiation into the idea that those in the spirit world can actually connect to us through our senses. This has been fairly rare for me, but there have been other times when I have awoken to the sound of my name being called, or to bells or gongs ringing; all fairly typical signs I discovered, of angels/spirit guides trying to get our attention. As I moved through my Reiki journey, there were times when I felt my hair being stroked. The intense tingles I would feel through my body, were for me, a sign that my sprit team were drawing close.

Throughout the last year, I have frequently experienced very intense energy around my right ear. The right side of our brain represents our creative side, and this energy seems to accompany the times I am writing this book. It leaves me in no doubt that I am getting a lot of help, downloads and assistance from the other side.

As far as Animal Communication is concerned, although I easily feel the physical sensations of the animal I am communicating with through my body, I had never experienced anything through my senses with an animal that was in spirit. Tess has been the first this has happened with. My experience with her was pretty incredible.

Tess, in her physical form had been a beautiful, black Labrador. She belonged to a friend of mine, who lived some distance away from me, but despite this, we always scheduled in an annual visit to my home, where my friend would bring Tess along too. We would have a lovely day walking her in the nearby beauty spot and having lunch together.

Even though I only saw Tess once a year, she would always come running up to my house when let out the car, greeting me warmly and excitedly. She was a truly beautiful, loving dog and was the apple of my friend's eyes. They experienced a very deep, close bond, so Caroline was understandably shattered when Tess developed a sudden untreatable spinal problem and had to be euthanized. She was only eight years old, and up until that point she had been the picture of health and fitness. It was a hard knock to take and Caroline struggled to come to terms with her untimely transition.

It was about eighteen months after her passing when Caroline asked me if I could please connect with Tess and pass on any messages she might have.

I was pretty busy at the time, but I promised I would try and connect with her in the next month. About a couple of weeks after making my promise, I had a very strange experience. I awoke suddenly at 12.00pm at night to the sound of a dog barking loudly in my ear. Although our neighbours have a dog, he is a small one and in any case, he never goes out at night. The volume of the bark left me in no doubt whatsoever that this was a dog from the spirit world. I immediately thought of my dog Candy who was in spirit, but the sound of this bark was nothing like her bark had been. It was loud and deep, and clearly belonged to a dog bigger than my miniature poodle. The bark echoed in my ears, and even when awake I could easily recall the depth, rhythm and quality of sound. I shrugged, rolled over and went back to sleep, having absolutely no idea why a dog would be waking me up in the middle of the night.

I thought no more of it until I connected with Tess a week later. She immediately reprimanded me with the time it had taken me to talk to her, and informed me that she thought the barking in my ear would remind me of the promise I had made to my friend. She had so much she wanted to pass on to Caroline that she couldn't wait to get started.

To say I was gobsmacked by this information is an understatement. My conscious mind had put the barking in the night to the back of my mind, so I was just astounded when Tess made this revelation. It felt a real privilege to have heard her in this way, and it was wonderful proof that those in spirit really can connect to us through our physical senses.

But Tess was going to take this physical connection one step further. I was going to experience something quite wonderful.

Before her final, beautiful gift, she had some lovely messages to pass on to her beloved owner. I have touched on some of these below, as I feel that the wisdom she passed on can help a lot of people who are grieving their lost loved ones.

Many people are left feeling extremely guilty when they decide to euthanise an animal. They agonise over whether it was the right time. Did they make the decision too hastily, or did they leave it too long? Over the years, I have experienced so many people torturing themselves over this decision.

Tess was now making it very clear that she wanted Caroline to stop feeling guilty about having her put to sleep. There is no right or wrong when it comes to making these decisions. If our actions are done with the very best intentions and with love in our heart, then the animal knows this and understands it was the right choice for them.

Tess was totally aware of the deep love Caroline felt for her and she was mirroring this right back. Even though she is in spirit, she still feels this energy, and it is the bridge that holds their hearts and souls together. She was eager to reassure Caroline that quality of life is way more important than quantity, and living a life filled with love and happiness is way superior to living a long life where physical pain would severely have reduced her ability to enjoy it.

She went on to explain that we decide before we come to Earth when we are to leave our body. Growing old, with its physical deterioration, is a lesson in itself, but she didn't need this lesson. Having been to Earth before, and having been through the physical degeneration lesson, it wasn't necessary for her to go through it again. Everything happened in perfect divine timing.

Many people also feel guilty about taking on another animal after their loved one has transitioned. They feel it could be seen as a betrayal, and their animal in spirit may be jealous. But, on the contrary, our animals rejoice that we are giving the chance for another animal to have a lovely home. Emotions like jealousy just don't exist in the afterlife.

So Tess proved this point when she expressed her delight that Caroline had taken on another dog, and was thinking of acquiring another. There are so many dogs needing good, loving homes, and not enough people who can provide everything a dog needs. Tess wanted to express her delight at this and she was smiling in Heaven for it.

I asked Tess what she spends time doing in Heaven. She explained that it is slightly different for dogs than it is for people. Whereas people have a lot of evolving to do, most dogs are pretty well already there – they understand so much already about giving unconditional love, compassion and empathy, as well as knowing how to live a joyful life (although obviously this can be somewhat constrained and controlled by their human caregivers). Dogs are God's gift to humans, helping them cope with life on Earth. They are also our teachers, giving us the opportunity to learn about giving love unconditionally, and helping to connect us to joy in the moment, and also to help connect us to the healing powers of nature. For many people, a dog's love is like no other. They provide comfort and learning at the same time. In this respect, dogs are like "Earth Angels" and make many peoples' lives easier.

So for dogs, Heaven is very different. Whereas humans carry on learning and developing, Heaven for dogs is very much about rejuvenation – taking the time to heal and come back to their love centre. Many dogs have had a very tough time on Planet Earth. And there are the minority who succumb to the negative vibrations of Earth. These are the ones that become unruly and aggressive. Many more are rejected, misunderstood and badly treated. These dogs are in desperate need of love and healing. Those dogs who had a better time of it like Tess, help and support the more unfortunate dogs. Tess helps with this. She showed me a beautiful picture of her running around beautiful flowers, with some of these "wounded dogs." Imagine all the things that dogs love doing best – that is what they do in Heaven. When they decide to return to Earth (and they often make this decision to help humans – either through offering comfort, services or for helping us with our spiritual development) they are given intensive training to help them cope to the best of their ability.

Tess was desperate for Caroline to not feel the grief of their parting. In Heaven you feel perpetual love and joy, and this is what all those in Heaven want for their beloved ones on Earth. They don't want to be missed or grieved. They want us to live in joy too and in so doing, we are honouring their memory. Also, love, joy and gratitude are the highest vibrations, so if we can achieve these states, then it gives those in Heaven the opportunity to draw close to us. They are around us all the time, but the only reason we can't normally see, hear or feel them, is because of the mismatch in our vibrational states. Those on Earth carry a lower vibration than those in Heaven. When we learn to increase our vibration, then it is easier to make contact.

Something else Tess mentioned was very interesting. In Heaven, there is no linear time or space, meaning that it is easy to move backwards or forwards in time. So Tess, if she chooses, can move forwards to a time when Caroline is with her. This is why those in Heaven don't miss the interactions they have with those they leave behind; for they can choose to move forward in time to be with their loved ones in a way where they can truly acknowledge each other. This is why it is only those of us left behind who feel the pain of a physical separation. Those in spirit don't experience this at all, because for them, there is no separation.

Finally, Tess gave me a song she wanted passing on to Caroline. Frequently, during my Animal Communication journey, I have received songs from the animal I have communicated with. This typically happens at the end of a reading when I ask if there is a message that they want to pass on to their Guardian. The way I understand this is as follows: the Universe selects a song on behalf of the animal which will convey the message they want to pass on. It nearly always corresponds with things the animal has expressed throughout the reading.

In the early days of carrying out communications, the songs appeared to me as music which started playing in my head, and they were tunes I recognised. But as I progressed with my readings, the title of a song would appear in my head. More often than not, these were songs I had never heard of, so I would have to Google them. I would always be amazed how much relevance these songs seemed to have to the conversation with the animal.

The song that Tess wanted to pass on to Caroline was entitled *"Just a Heartbeat Away."* I had never heard of a song with this title, but like all the others before, I found it did exist and was sung by Scott Johnson. In fact, the theme of the song was absolutely spot on with the messages Tess had been passing on. She really wanted Caroline to appreciate the wonder of her new life, and she wanted to reassure her that even though she can't be seen, she is still by her side whenever she needs her. It is a truly beautiful song, and there is a lovely video accompanying it. The words were exactly what Caroline needed to hear.

The animals have led me to some truly beautiful songs, and this was another one to add to my growing list. I really urge you to check it out and watch the video, as the message is exactly what our loved ones in spirit want us to know. If you are like me, it is probably best to have a tissue handy, as the song really touches your soul. It is a very catchy song too, so you will probably be singing it for the rest of the day. Be warned!

So, to the final, beautiful gift! When I asked Tess if there was anything she wanted to gift to Caroline, I instantly felt a very strange tingling sensation move from my bottom left jaw up to the brow of my head. I asked Tess what on Earth that was, and she informed me that she had just given me the biggest, sloppiest, wet kiss she could muster. Quite understandably, I was not the intended recipient. It was to be passed on to my friend! Frankly, I was just in awe. This was something never before experienced, and it felt amazing. How wonderful to feel this physical sensation across the spiritual divide. Oh, the possibilities! When we open up to these connections, life just becomes so magical. Sometimes I could just cry with the wonder of it all.

I thanked Tess for communicating so clearly, and promised to pass her messages and gifts on to my friend. It had been a magical experience for all of us.

A self-reflection exercise

- Have the intention to connect with one of your animals in spirit. If it helps, hold their photograph in front of you and connect with the essence of their Being.

- Make sure there are no distractions and you won't be disturbed.

- Start to connect to your breath, taking deep breaths in through the nose, and out through the mouth.

- Start to think of your animal in spirit, and really focus on the good times you shared with them. Let your heart expand with love and imagine yourself surrounded by a beautiful white light. Picture your animal reaching out to you through this light, and imagine a rainbow bridge stretching from your heart to theirs. Try calling them to you, just as you would have done when they were on the physical plane.

- Ask them to allow you to feel their presence. Be very quiet and still for the next ten minutes and just feel into the connection you have created. Can you smell, hear or see them? Can you sense their presence, or even feel them? You may feel tingles or parts of your body may go hot or cold. Do you feel any sensations in your body? Just become super-aware of any of these things, because your animal will do everything in their power to let you know that they are by your side.

- Remember to thank your animal for allowing this connection to be forged and be immensely grateful for them reaching out to you in this way.

AFTERWORD - AWAKEN TO THE MAGIC

Just because someone tells you that something isn't real, doesn't make it a truth. It might be for them, but not necessarily for you. If we live in a vibrating Universe that responds to our thoughts, feelings and emotions, then a belief in magic and miracles is going to bring them to your door. It is a Universal Law! This is now my truth and I am living it.

As I step out of the car, the sound of Jazz neighing resounds in my ears. It is less of a welcoming call; more of a *"Can you please release me?"* refrain.

Sure enough, the moment she spots me, her body language along with her vocal whinnying, is making it very clear that she is regarding me as her rescuer. *"Can you please let me out of this stable!"* she is screaming.

There is one significant problem. The ground is covered with ice and snow. It is absolutely treacherous! Just walking from my car to the barn has required me to use all my focus to stay on my feet. Leading the horses down the path to their field is simply out of the question; not if we want our horses to remain in one piece.

This is the second day that the horses have been imprisoned in their stable, and Jazz is quite simply not a happy horse. Although content to come into her stable at night, for her, twenty-four hours imprisonment is a step too far. And now we had far exceeded even twenty-four hours.

I totally empathised with her frustration. Being stuck in a 12ft square room would have me climbing the walls too. But better a bored/frustrated horse than an injured or dead one.

I apologised to Jazz and explained why she needed to spend another day in her stable. *"Ok"* she replied, *"But at least let me stretch my legs."*

How could I refuse? It seemed like a perfectly reasonable request, so I slipped her headcollar on, ensuring that the barriers were placed on the outside doors, and proceeded to lead her around the roomy barn.

It started off fine. Jazz was thankful to relieve her stiff legs, so she walked around the fairly large barn quite happily. But then she wanted more, and that "more" to her meant venturing outside.

Feeling her mounting energy, I recognised that it was essential to get her back into the stable before her adrenaline overthrew me.

Jazz was not happy to be returned to her prison, but in spite of that, she did walk in without protest. I quickly pushed the bolt across the closing door because I knew what would happen next.

Sure enough, Jazz could no longer contain her adrenaline. Whizzing around the stable, she was threatening to come over the stable door. How could I help her? I knew there was only one solution.

It was of vital importance that I disconnected from her hysteria, so standing outside her stable, I breathed deeply and disassociated from what was playing out in front of me. Finding my calm was paramount. If I was to help Jazz, then I needed to focus on my own energy. The moment I started to feel the tingle of Reiki energy, I began directing it towards her. As the tendrils of the peaceful, calming energy reached out to her, even I was shocked at the speed of Jazz's reaction. For in just a few short minutes she was standing at the back of the stable yawning her head off. I must have witnessed at least ten huge, deep yawns.

Grabbing my phone out my pocket, I attempted to video this release. There were no more yawns, but Jazz was now the picture of an incredibly calm, peaceful horse; a complete contrast to the crazed horse of just a few minutes earlier.

Don't ask me why I chose to video her. This is not something I normally do, yet weirdly on this occasion I seemed compelled to video my now utterly chilled horse. But why? Maybe the answer lies in what showed up in that video. I may have missed the yawns, but I had captured something far more intriguing.

Whilst filming the two minute video, I was aware of coloured lights flitting around the viewfinder, but my logical mind was informing me that it must have something to do with the light catching the dust in the stable and illuminating it. I scarcely paid it any attention.

It was only when I played the video back (immediately after filming it) that my attention was well and truly piqued. For the moving balls of light looked distinctively like orbs. Not only that, but there were just hundreds of them – different sizes, varying colours, and moving in different directions. Some appeared very large indeed, and others were more like small balls of light dancing around Jazz's feet.

I ran around to Rosie's stable, situated in the barn behind Jazz's stable, and pressed the video button on my camera. I captured a few, a couple which were very impressive.

Downloading the videos on to my computer at home, there was no doubt in my mind that these were indeed orbs – and very impressive ones they were too.

It did make perfect sense. When carrying out Reiki healing, I always call upon angels and spirit guides for help. Orbs are presumed to be non-physical entities, so could these Beings have come in to help with the healing? Did they represent physical proof that I was indeed receiving the assistance that I was calling in? Just the thought left me feeling excited. I felt full of awe and gratitude for the heavenly assistance, particularly as Jazz continued to remain serene and calm for the rest of the day. Would it last?

Arriving at the yard the following morning, I discovered a very different Jazz to the one from the morning before. She whinnied softly, before returning to munching her haylage. Was this even the same horse?

I decided not to attempt taking her out the stable, risking giving her false hope of time in her field, so I chose to muck out around her instead. Jazz showed not even the remotest interest in escaping from her stable. It seemed that she had very much come to terms with her stable confinement and she was going to make the most of what fate had handed her. The noise of her munching on her haylage was very comforting.

Late morning, it was decided that it was safe enough for some horses to be led to their field. Temperatures had warmed a little and the ice had melted sufficiently for some of the fields to be accessed without it being an act of jeopardy. Sadly, this was not true of Jazz's and Rosie's field. For them, it was still too risky to venture out.

This presented a new dilemma. The horses around Jazz were all to be put out, which potentially would be very upsetting for her. She wouldn't be happy that she was expected to remain in her stable while those around her were gaining their freedom. What to do?

The answer was obvious: Jazz would need some more reiki. This time I carried it out in the stable while Jazz was eating her hay. Unbelievably, as the horses around her were being led out, Jazz didn't even look up from her hay net. She cared not a jot!

After ten minutes of letting the Reiki flow, Jazz once again took herself to the back of the stable, releasing those huge yawns. I pressed the video button on my phone. Would the orbs appear again?

They did not disappoint. Like the day before, the three minute video featured hundreds of different sized, coloured orbs. It was a repeat performance of the day before.

This time though I carried out a short experiment. Ten minutes after closing the Reiki session down, I took another video. Jazz was still standing in the same spot in her stable, and I was in the same position as before. Jazz's stable was right at the back of the barn, so there was no natural light, but I made sure that the same lights were turned on.

The result? Not a single orb to be found. Just as the Reiki energy had dissipated, so had the orbs. What better proof that the orbs were indeed connected to the Reiki energy?

But there was more proof to come, A couple of hours later, the ice had melted sufficiently to make it safe enough to put Jazz and Rosie in their field. As an extra precaution, Lauren and I took shovels down to the field, breaking and clearing away any remaining ice. We now had an ice free pathway to the field.

I spoke to Jazz, explaining to her that she needed to be very slow and careful on the walk down to her field. No crazy shenanigans! It was important that she listened to me every step of the way.

Don't ever accuse your horse of not listening. From the very first step out of her stable, Jazz was the perfect representation of calm. She listened to me every step of the way, walking slowly and sedately down the path, as we wove our way around the icy patches. Her normal bouncy self was nowhere to be seen.

I should have had the same chat with Rosie, as this normally placid horse, was dancing, and prancing behind us, while Lauren hung gainly on to her rope.

I marvelled at how quietly Jazz had walked out for me. So much so that she resembled a horse who had been sedated. Even on her release into the field, she ignored Rosie's request to *"Let's go crazy."* Leaving Rosie to gallop and buck around the field on her own, Jazz quietly tucked into her haylage.

This filming of the orbs took place in early December 2022. Over Christmas, there were many gatherings with family and friends, so I was able to show my orb videos to a fair number of people. Most, were understandably very quizzical, believing them to be dust particles illuminated by the light - the common explanation for orb phenomena.

I do get this. We are so trained in rational/logical thinking, that it can be very hard to perceive things any other way. I too was once the same! But having experienced so much over the last 11 years that defies rational thinking, I no longer perceive that way. I am so much more open to the magic of divinity all around us, and most days I am awed by the mystery and beauty of life. Once you have seen the magic, there is no unseeing it. It is as simple as that!

So the scepticism just made me more determined than ever to prove that these beautiful orbs in my videos were manifestations of something extraordinary. I fervently believed that healing non- physical entities had been giving me a hand, and I was determined to prove it.

My interest in the subject led me to a fascinating book, *"Orbs: Their Mission and Messages of Hope."* The physicist who authored the book, Klaus Heinemann, is a leading expert on orbs, having studied, photographed and conducted World Conferences on them. There are so many amazing photos of them in his book. His work led him to an astounding conclusion – they are representative of healing non-physical entities, and they are very much connected to the consciousness of a healer.

Furthermore, I discovered that my orbs did seem to reflect the unique properties which genuine orbs possess. They were of varying sizes, different colours, moving in random directions and some would materialise out of the middle of the screen, appearing to emanate out of Jazz herself. Some moved at incredibly fast speeds, and others behaved in a quantum manner, disappearing and then reappearing again.

I must have studied my orb videos for months, slowing down the videos and creating photos of them. If you check out my blog, *"Miracle at Christmas"* on my website (www.unitingsouls.com) you will see some of the photos I created from the videos.

If you are still unconvinced, consider this. Orbs are typically picked up on photos as opposed to videos, because it is the flash on the camera which captures them. So it is rare to see orbs on videos. Also, the shutter speed on my phone camera is slow, and is not set up to capture orbs.

Perhaps the most compelling evidence, is that, despite trying to create conditions which would capture a dust orb, I have completely failed to do so. I have emptied shavings in the stable, created dust in my house, and taken videos/photos in these recommended conditions, but I have failed to capture a single one.

All this has led me to the conclusion that something very magical indeed occurred in December 2022, and having the physical evidence of it leaves me incredibly awed and grateful. It is a true gift from spirit!

I have included this story here, to demonstrate how Animal Communication is just one step towards a very magical journey. I believe that divine help is very much part and parcel of these practices. The Universe not only helps convert what the animals want to say into a language we can understand, but is also empowering the healing work we conduct. It is humbling to recognise that our deeper understanding of our animals is enabled by this divine help.

So what of the future? As I write this, there are gigantic steps being made forward in the field of consciousness. Particularly poignant is the fact that the 2022 Nobel Physics prize-winners were three Quantum physicists for their work on "entanglement." To be a Nobel prize winner, you have to have more than a theory- it has to be proven as fact. So, their work has effectively proven that far from being separated from each other, we are all very much connected to each other as part of a greater whole. The reality we have been basing our thoughts and beliefs on has been completely overturned. Yet interestingly, the media has been remarkably quiet about this.

I love that science and spirituality are beginning to merge, and it leaves me optimistic that we can look forward to a future that combines knowledge with wisdom – something which is very much needed if we are to create a better world, or indeed, any world at all. For if we continue on our current trajectory, we are doomed.

But the forerunners to this "New World" are the animals themselves. They are the ones who remind us to open our hearts and to connect to our inner joy. They are the ones who are cracking us open and gently encouraging us to return to our true, divine nature. Through their own pure, innate nature, unsullied by materialism, greed and the sense of self, they are demonstrating how we should be living our lives. They have never lost their connection to nature and Mother Earth. They have never become so disassociated from themselves that they don't even know who they are any more. But we have. And it is the animals who want to get us back on track, reminding us that we have a great responsibility, not only to them and the Earth, but to ourselves too. If life is to continue on this planet, then we have to awaken, and elevate ourselves to a much higher level of consciousness.

The animals are talking and helping us awaken. We just need to listen!

ABOUT THE AUTHOR

Following her spiritual awakening in 2012, Fiona became passionate about helping give animals a voice. It was them, after all, who had created the huge shift in her life.

She learned everything she could about Animal Communication and became a Master Reiki Healer.

In February 2024, she gave up her tax job to devote herself wholly to her Animal Communication and reiki work, and she started a business focusing on these areas.

Her other books published to date are: -

Seeker of the Light

A Horse's Voice

Fiona can be contacted as follows: -

Website: https://unitingsouls.co.uk

Facebook Page: Uniting Souls through Animal Communication and Reiki Healing

Email address: fiona.sutton@btinternet.com

Printed in Great Britain
by Amazon